DECE

DECEIVED

Bonnie Woods

Typeset by Avocet Typeset, Chilton, Aylesbury, Bucks
Printed in England by J F Print Ltd, Sparkford, Somerset

Contents

Foreword

There is an advertisement that offers help for motorists in trouble with their car but cannot find help. The punch line comes when the voice over tells us that he doesn't know much about cars," … but I know a man who does." I would paraphrase that a little. I have never been involved in Scientology, never experienced the pressure of maintaining the huge demands some religious groups place upon their adherents-but I know a woman who has!

Bonnie Woods attended the church at which I was then pastor. She came as she will explain, because one of her daughters was involved in our youth work-for me it was a lovely serendipity. This was one of those things God does in our lives to enrich us and challenge us. He did just that by enriching me as a pastor with a family who really believed His word and lived as though they believed it. They believed what His word, the Bible states even when insurmountable odds appeared to be stacked against them. Here is a family who take His word literally, so when he said *"And I will lead the blind in a way that they know not, in paths that they have not known I will guide them. I will turn the darkness before them into light, the rough places into level ground. These are the things I will do, and I will not forsake them." Isaiah 42:16(RSV)* – For them that was gospel and God has proved it to be so.

This family challenged me. Not by any direct words, but by living out their faith. I look around the world today and see some of the terrible injustices and persecutions, all the time wondering how people of faith continue in those circumstances. I look at the Christians we have in government today and wonder how they manage to go on from day to day in spite of the awful things that are said about them in the media, but somehow they manage to come back with a smile and a word devoid of malice. I see that in the Woods family. As you read through the following pages you may think something Bonnie has written is unfair, unreasonable, or even unjust; just keep this in mind will you, she lived it. She has been there, done it, and has the T shirt to prove it. Bonnie and Richard deserve to be heard. Listen, and see if like me you are not enriched by tracing the steps of this family through their experience of trusting the Lord God, see, if like me, you are challenged to take His word more seriously than you may have done previously.

Charles Crane
August 2003
Dorchester

"Fear not and be not dismayed at this great multitude, for the battle is not yours, but God's."
2 Chronicles 20:15 (RSV)

Chapter One

Labelled and Libelled

'Want a cup of coffee Mum?' inquired my daughter Desiree as she opened the fridge door to get out some milk. 'Oh, hang on though, I'll have to see if it's arrived – we've run out' she added quickly, as she rushed to the front door before I had a chance to answer her question.

The early morning routine was kicking in like it did most weekdays. I had got up at my normal time, and had started to fix breakfast. My younger daughter Andreanna was still to surface and meanwhile the television was mumbling away in the background, with a commercial break clamouring for attention every ten minutes or so. The TV was tuned to an early morning news programme interspersed with travel reports and showbiz items. All I wanted to know was what the weather was going to do. England was very unlike my own country of the United States, where we never had to think too much about what the weather was going to be like on any given day. As long as we knew what season we were in, we roughly knew what kind of day to expect. Although it was an early June morning, I felt a draught from the front door. How long did it take, I wondered impatiently, for a teenage girl to bring in two bottles of milk? Maybe she had stopped to chat to my husband Richard who was up and about somewhere, maybe encouraging Andreanna to get a move on. Although he was British through and through he had spent some time in the States, where we had met and married, so we both understood enough about each other's cultures to get along well.

Desiree suddenly reappeared, looking upset. 'What's wrong honey' I said, trying to think what could have made her look so distressed, having gone no further than the front door.

'You're not going to believe this Mum,' she said, plonking the milk bottles on the work surface, and staring hard at a piece of paper in her hand. 'It's horrible!' 'What is?' I said, suddenly feeling disturbed, without knowing why, 'please give it to me'.

She handed it over, still looking concerned, and then she turned away and started to open one of the bottles. I took what looked like a newsletter from her, and to my surprise saw a picture of myself with the words Hate Campaigner emblazoned underneath. I felt dumb with shock. How dare they! I knew immediately who was responsible. This was the work of the Church of Scientology. The Scientologists hated anyone messing in their affairs, and I had begun trying to warn people about the dangers of getting involved in their organisation as I had once been for some years. Their way of defending their beliefs was to go on the attack as hard as they could.

'Was this thing pushed through the letter box' I said to Desiree.

'No, it was lodged in between the milk bottles' she said tearfully. 'Oh Mum, this is just horrible'.

She started to cry, and I wanted to as well. But I felt too angry to cry. Now I wasn't safe from their grip, even in my own home. I began to read beyond the offending header to the main body of the text. I quickly saw that it was alleging that Escape, the counselling service that I had started to help those who wanted to get free from the entanglements of the Scientologists was just a front for a 'deprogramming' organisation which tried to force people away from their chosen faith by brainwashing. It suggested that I had come to East Grinstead to wage a campaign of hatred and discrimination against religious groups. It went on to say that I falsely and hypocritically claimed to be a born again Christian in order to facilitate my campaign of hatred and discrimination, and that my actions were motivated by hatred and religious intolerance.

As I read the offensive and distorted spiel that had upset my daughter so much, the things that I had suffered at the hands of the Scientologist movement over many years flashed across my mind. I remembered how they had made contact with me at a time of great vulnerability in my life, and how after I had showed an interest in their methods they had gradually sucked me into their net, so that in the end I wasn't free to think or act without their agreement. I recalled the long hard hours of mind numbing work for little or no pay, how I was punished if I didn't fulfil their impossible quotas, and how, in trying to do so, I forfeited valuable time with my infant daughter, who they disturbed then, just as they were upsetting her now, many years later. Then other incidents that I had endured at their hand started to surface in my mind, but I refused myself the indulgence of dwelling on them at this moment. 'I've been abused, robbed and deceived' I thought, trying not to get angry, 'so just when are they going to stop hounding me?'

Suddenly my thoughts and my unanswered question were interrupted by a knock on the door. Richard, who had joined me in the kitchen, shut the kitchen door before he answered the front door. I could hear him speaking quietly to one of our neighbours. It seemed as though the conversation was over almost before it had begun, and then he returned carrying another copy of the leaflet. He explained that the next door neighbour had brought it round thinking that he'd better let us know he'd received it. I started to cry as he explained that other neighbours had received the leaflet as well. I wasn't sure if I was crying because I was angry or embarrassed. This unpleasant incident, coming as it did at the beginning of the day, made us all wonder what to do next. Andreanna made her entrance, looking sleepy and then puzzled at our glum faces. I put her in the picture as calmly and quickly as I could, not wanting her to be upset at the very start of her day. Then after a few minutes chatting together we all decided that it would be best if the girls went to school as normal, united in the idea that we didn't want to change any of our schedules to suit our tormentor's tactics.

After the girls had left the house I read the leaflet again in more detail. It seemed to be implying that I was some kind of religious bigot, who did not want people to believe anything other than what I believed! Nothing in fact could have been further from the truth. As an American, I believed firmly in the freedom of speech, and the right for everyone to practise whatever religion they felt was appropriate for them. I was in fact the child of a 'mixed' marriage, my mother being Protestant and my father a Catholic. I too had been associated with the Catholic Church for many years, before getting involved with Scientology. It was only through God's grace that I had finally heard the Gospel message and responded to it, which gave to me strength to break with the Scientologists. And it was because of the control and domination that seemed to hold the organisation

4

together that I wanted to at least warn people of what they potentially could be getting into.

About mid-morning the doorbell went again. It was our good friend Tony Hennell. He didn't waste any time in telling us that he and his wife Mandy had received one of the offending leaflets too. This was getting serious. Tony and Mandy lived a few streets away from our house in East Grinstead, so the fact that they had had one also made me wonder just how many houses had been targeted. It was possible that the whole of the town had been covered. The Scientologists were a powerful enough organisation to do that if they wanted to. And the chances were that many people would read it, because it looked at first glance like a newsletter, with the heading Religious Freedom News – Issue 1.

But informing us of the leaflet was not the only reason for Tony's visit. He was there because Richard and I had agreed to go with him to attend a vigil outside the Scientology bookshop in the East Grinstead High Street that morning. The shock of seeing my name and photograph with the words Hate Campaigner had deeply upset me, and I had temporarily forgotten our plans for the day. But I now felt determined that although the leaflet was probably designed to scare me off, I was not going to be bullied. After a strong cup of coffee, and a quick prayer, we all made our way to the bookshop, arriving about 11 o'clock.

As soon as we arrived we donned badges which read Christian Vigil Against Scientology and started to walk up and down outside the shop, praying as we did so. Before long we were joined by two other friends of ours, Hazel and Paula. Although the High Street was fairly busy, no one showed any interest in actually going into the shop. However, a Scientologist was positioned outside the premises, holding a clipboard, and trying to get people interested in taking a personality test, a scheme they often used to have initial contact with the general public. If any of the people that he approached took a leaflet, we would offer them one of ours which was entitled What the Scientologists Don't Tell You. Thinking about the problems I had had with this organisation, it was very important to me that anyone who was potentially going to get involved with them made an informed decision. I suppose I was partially motivated by a strong need to redress the shame I felt at having recruited so many hundreds of people during the time I worked for them.

By the end of the morning I gave out about three or four leaflets, and I reckon about a dozen leaflets were given out by us all in total.

But I had only been outside the shop for about half an hour when several Scientologists arrived in a kind of jeep. A woman jumped out, stood in front of the bookstore and held a copy of the Hate Campaigner leaflet above her head. At this point, I was standing near the kerb by the bookshop and a man who worked for a printing company who had connections with Scientology was talking to me. I hadn't given him one of our leaflets, because he knew about Scientology already.

As we talked, several of the Scientologists came and stood very close to me. They started shouting things like 'Hey, this is the woman' and 'Have you seen what she has done'. I felt threatened by their behaviour, as they stood there, each of them clutching a large number of leaflets. Then the women, who the others called Sheila put her face very close to mine and said 'This leaflet is just the first – there are going to be others' She stood so close that I felt her breath on my face, and saw the hatred in her eyes. My friends, Hazel and Paula joined me, and tried to protect me from the other Scientologists. Richard then took control, asking them to move back, and when they refused, he took me away from them. We walked to the other side of the street, and away from their threatening behaviour. I wanted to be brave, but again I felt very upset.

The fact that we had now walked away from the shop didn't make them calm down in any way. They were holding the Hate Campaigner leaflet above their heads and shouting to anyone who would listen 'Look, this is the woman in the pamphlets' and 'Have you seen this woman'. Not content with that, they started to put the leaflet through the open car windows of vehicles waiting at the traffic lights, and one of the Scientologists even got on to a bus, and started to hand out the leaflets to the passengers!

Then a fairly tall man with reddish hair and eyes that seemed to bore into me followed us across the road, pointing and shouting at us. He stopped following us when Richard threatened to perform a Citizens Arrest on him, but immediately another man, younger than the first, probably in his twenties I guessed, who they called Nick, started to follow us. He came up to me a couple of times, shoving the leaflet in front of my face and shouting to passers-by. All the shouting and jostling made me feel very afraid. They seemed to be acting out of so much hatred and hostility, and were trying to distribute as many of their leaflets about me as possible. As we made our way back home, I wondered just what would happen next. I knew that now they had targeted us, there would be no stopping them.

Richard and I spent the next few days praying hard and thinking what the next course of action should be. After showing the offending leaflet to a friend of ours who was in the legal profession, who in turn showed it to someone she knew who specialised in libel matters, we finally decided that, rightly or wrongly, the only thing to do was to issue a writ against the Scientologists for libel. We were concerned that the truth should be told in the hope that it would encourage other former members to stand up for their right to speak out about their own experiences. I knew that issuing a writ would be a very costly decision and guessed that we were probably only at the tip of an iceberg of harassment. Subsequent events proved my fears to be depressingly correct.

We heard from some old friends and neighbours of ours that someone claiming to be a detective from America had been knocking on their doors, asking questions about us. This man had obviously discovered all the addresses we had lived at in the past.

It didn't take him long to discover that Richard had been made bankrupt, following an unwise business deal that had caused him great hassle, cost him a great deal of money and lots of heartache. The private detective discovered all the addresses that we had lived at in the past, knocked on the door of adjoining houses, and asked the people living there if they knew of us. If they said that they did, he told them that he was a detective from America, omitting the word private making his visit sound official. Most of the people he contacted naturally assumed that he was a policeman. He would start by asking if he could have a private word with them as he was trying to find out about some stolen documents, but once he was invited inside their homes, he would start to talk about Richard's bankruptcy and whatever else he had found out to discredit us in the eyes of our former neighbours, as well as our present day friends and fellow church members.

Some, without realising what they were doing, would say things to him in all innocence, which added to his information about us, or his list of contacts. Finally he had quite a few things which made us look as though we were dishonest, and after he filed his report to the Scientologists, they put all the details in their newspaper which is ironically called Freedom, which was then distributed across the length and breath of the United Kingdom. The article included photos of us, which they had obtained through video surveillance. The next thing we knew, the people that he had interviewed also received a copy of the newspaper! Some of our friends told us what they had received, and were very supportive towards us. But it was odd, and unpleasant, to be recognised by someone in a shop, knowing that the newspaper was probably the sole the source of their information about us.

I was in a grocery store soon after the newspaper had been distributed, and I heard a woman who was standing behind me whisper to her husband 'I think that's her – the one we saw in the newspaper'. Without thinking, and much to her surprise, I turned around and said 'If you have a copy, I'll autograph it for you!'

On another occasion Richard and I were in London – we had been demonstrating against the Scientologists outside their London Headquarters, along with a group of friends we had made contact with through the Internet who were protesting about the harassment other critics had suffered. Desiree who was 17 and Andreanna who had just turned 11 were quite happy to be left at home for the day, and we told them approximately the time they could expect us home, before rushing out of the house to catch the train to London. After the demonstration was over we went into a pub for a drink before going home, and a Scientology Intelligence Agent followed us in, and came and sat right next to me. I knew exactly who he was because each time we were involved in a demonstration against Scientology this guy from the Office of Special Affairs was usually assigned to take our photographs – but not content with that, he would then follow us to the pub where we used to congregate after the demonstrations. It was an odd relationship he had with him, because he knew how much against Scientology we were, yet he would always refer to us by our first names, and seemed genuinely interested in our views about Scientology.

'Why are you doing all this Bonnie?' was his surprising question to me that day. 'Why are you so upset?'

'Well I just don't think you should harass people who have a different viewpoint from your own' I told him.

I then started to tell him about a friend of ours, Jon Atack, who had written a book about the dangers of Scientology called A Piece of Blue Sky which had helped me tremendously in sorting myself out, after leaving the Scientologists. Jon had had a Scientologist demonstration outside his home, with placards and the rest, which had really upset his five year old daughter, to the point where she had scrawled on a piece of paper the words Please Go Away and held it up at the window.

'So, demonstrations outside peoples homes are something that I feel you should just not do' I said in conclusion, hoping that he might start to grasp how dreadful it was to have to go through something like that.

'Oh, that's very interesting,' was his only comment. I should have known better than to say what I did. He grasped the implications of what I had told him all too well – and put them into immediate effect!

After our drink, we left the pub and made out way back to Victoria Station to catch the train home, not having a clue as to what my brief conversation had set in motion. Then, just as we were getting on the train, I noticed that the same man I had talked to in the pub was now in a phone booth, watching which train we were boarding.

When we arrived back to East Grinstead, we left the station, jumped into the car and started to drive home. But as we approached the area in which we lived, we suddenly saw a group of children on bikes coming towards us, waving their arms and shouting. It was a bit like a scene from the film ET! They made it clear that they wanted us to stop, and when we did we realised that they were friends of our two girls.

'Go home quick,' they said excitedly, 'terrible things are happening at your house. There are people there with signs, and your girls are really scared'.

Without asking any more questions, we thanked the children, and sped home as fast as the law allowed. We arrived to see about half a dozen people marching up and down outside our house with placards. A father of one of the girls' neighbourhood friends who we had never met, was standing just inside the front door, with a protective arm around Andreanna. As I hurried to reach the girls I was taunted with shouts of 'Did you have a good time in London?' The father, introduced himself and said he had been reluctant to leave the girls as he felt the mood of the crowd outside was angry and ugly.

Richard was so incensed that he went inside and called the police, and asked them to have the people removed. The answer that he got was surprising. Because it was a peaceful demonstration the police told him there was nothing that they could do about it. The demonstrators had the law on their side!

But then our friends and neighbours started to ring the police to support our complaints, and eventually the demonstrators moved off, but not before they had made the point that they knew what our weakness was, and were more than willing to exploit it.

The harassment didn't stop there. A few weeks later I was in Chelsea, walking a friend to the tube station, when suddenly I was confronted by a very tall, well built man who I had never seen before, with all manner of fancy cameras hanging from a leather belt and slung over his shoulder who began to take several photographs of me. Again, trying to get out of a humiliating and embarrassing situation using humour, I turned my head away from him and said 'Look, if you're going to do this, could you please take me them from my left side, I prefer that profile!'

I guess I sounded casual, but in fact I felt really intimidated. But I was also determined not to be scared to the point that I didn't feel safe in going out without Richard's protection. What kind of life would that be? But the truth was that they were starting to grind me down.

I made a mental list of what we had endured in the recent past. A private detective was trying to rake up as much from the past as he could. Our house was marked out, and sometimes demonstrations were held outside. Phone calls then started to come through from the people the private detective had been in touch with, telling us the kind of questions they had been asked by him.

What tactic would they try next, I wondered as I snuggled down in bed one chilly night some time later. A further unpleasant incident had taken place that day when another complete stranger had popped out of nowhere, stood in front of me, produced a camera and took a photograph before disappearing into the crowd once more.

I felt a cold shiver go down my spine which had nothing to do with the temperature of the room. Far from things coming to an end, I suspected that this was just the beginning. There was far more to come, I felt sure of that.

Chapter Two

An Afternoon To Remember

'Bonnie, you've got to stop your mind from wandering' I told myself, as I gazed at the brightly coloured swings and slides in the playground, waiting as they were under a cloudless sky for their users to come and claim them once more. It was a hot Friday afternoon in 1973, when nothing much was going on, and things were slowing down for the weekend. I watched as a butterfly delicately landed on a leaf, before flying off again, like a small fragile animated feather, yet with a life and destiny all of its own. I casually wondered what it must be like to be absolutely free to fly wherever one wanted to go, helped by the soft summer breeze. I turned and looked around at the children in the room, all busy with their assignments, accompanied by that gentle murmur made by children who are concentrating hard. I had found a moment's peace in the midst of a hectic day as the kids busied themselves with paper, glitter and glue. My classroom was just one of many in a huge brick building standing in lovely grounds. I always felt fortunate that I had such a good view from its huge wooden sash windows. I found my eyes being drawn again to the scene outside. But I knew that I shouldn't stare out of the window when working. After all, I had a class to run – and not an easy one either. It wasn't the kids fault – they all had special needs, which is why they were at this Catholic boarding school in St Louis, Missouri run by the Notre Dame nuns where I had taught for several years now. I knew I was fortunate to get the job – I wasn't exactly a model Catholic. I was divorced from my first husband, and didn't come from a traditional Catholic family background either.

My childhood was happy enough though, in fact it wouldn't be an overstatement to say that it was idyllic. When I was about two years old my parents had purchased a plot of land in the heart of the Ohio countryside and Dad proceeded to build the house that my mother had designed. The back garden contained about an acre of locust trees and an apple orchard that spilled down the hillside into a huge state park that encompassed the winding Cuyahoga River, giving the park its aptly named title of the Emerald Necklace.

Mom was a Protestant and had to sign an agreement to raise any children that she had as Catholics before she could marry Dad. But Mom being Mom had her own way of sticking to her agreement – like leaving out the doctrinal points that she thought I and my three elder sisters didn't need to know! In spite of that I ended up making a prayer closet out of a walk-in clothes cupboard, with a glow in the dark statue of Jesus that I had won years before in a competition, which cast a strange eerie light on me as I held deep conversations with Him each day.

Family pets played a big part in my childhood. There was an Irish setter called Riley, a Persian cat, two very large rabbits – and a sheep called Babbet! But it was the horses that I probably spent the most time with. Each morning, after swallowing cereal as quickly as we could, my sisters and I would roam the local countryside in search of adventure. No one seemed too worried about our safety or what time we would return as long as my sisters promised to keep me in close tow. Occasionally my sister Cherie would let us ride the two horses down to the river for a swim. The small barn at the back of the property was where they were stabled and they were the passion and focus of a lot of Cherie's time.

As the youngest of four daughters and with a seven year gap between my sister Amy's birthday and mine, I had the benefit of my mother's undivided attention during the school terms. Consequently when I did finally arrive at the small Catholic grade school we all attended I was already reading and writing and was less than impressed with what was on offer for at least the first couple of years.

From the start of the first grade I had attended Catholic schools. One such school, run by the Sisters of St. Joseph, had my eldest sister Denise in the convent as a nun, so a special eye was kept on me by the other sisters. Mom started to tutor a few private students in Latin and French once I started school, and so was well able to satisfy the interest I had in the meanings of all the Latin words that I heard at Mass, causing me and my other two older sisters Cherie and Amy to become pretty steeped in the Catholic faith in spite of Mom's previous precautions. I had a wonderfully protected, sheltered childhood, and maybe the absence of any hardship or suffering in my early years made me pretty naïve about life or the possibility that I could be deceived or tricked into compromising what I believed.

My mother always said that hindsight gives us 20/20 vision, so I'm not sure if, had I been more street-wise, I might have made different choices about joining a cult later on. It begs the question about whether or not we can offer our children some explanation about the possibility of a group having a hidden agenda and their need to critically consider any invitations to give up your life to a group, even if it's only a little bit at a time.

Following high school, I chose the comfortable option of a small girls college operated by the same order of nuns. I left home for the first time and travelled what felt like a world away to where I now found myself – St. Louis, Missouri. I was hopelessly homesick for the first year and couldn't seem to settle on one particular course of study to take up as a major subject. I switched from Speech Therapy to studying to becoming a teacher of children with special needs. This choice required a study of psychology but I was allowed to select a minor study of English Literature.

I met my first husband, David at a college dance in the beginning of my second year at college. To my parent's dismay I decided to quit school so that we could get married right away. I had also made up my mind that I should find a full time job so that David could finish his degree in city planning. But that was the beginning of a season of tears, as I quickly began to realize that our marriage was falling apart, and I hadn't a clue about what I could do to repair the growing rift between us. We had known each other such a short time when we had committed ourselves to such an important a thing as married life together.

They say that you never really know someone until you marry them, and that was certainly the case as far as David was concerned. He was tall and muscular, and although he was never physically violent towards me, on several occasions he displayed violent outbursts, which in my mind was like living with a human volcano because I never knew when the next eruption was about to take place! I was too young and inexperienced to know how to deal with these incidents, or to know where to go for help. But once the trust between us started to erode, so sadly did our marriage. It was only after we had separated that I discovered that David had been married some years previous to our meeting, before having this first marriage annulled by the Catholic church. So I began to realise that our marriage had never been founded on a basis of truth and openness which is essential to make any relationship work.

But that was some years ago. I was now 25, and although I had a failed marriage behind me, I now had a nice boyfriend called Larry who was really keen to get on and improve himself – and me too, if I wanted. Strangely enough it was through David that Larry and I first met.

They say that men who feel violent towards their wives have a tendency to buy them expensive presents, and David one day announced that he wanted to buy me a new car. I fell in love with the BMW sports car he purchased for me immediately, loving its gorgeous shiny yellow paintwork. What I didn't realise was that while I was looking at the car, Larry, the car mechanic) was thinking that he would like to know me a little better! So some time later when I brought the car in for a service he asked me out for a date. I was young and lonely – and because David was working every night I was also bored, and that's how our relationship started. Some time later when things between David and I started to get really difficult I left home and started to live with Larry.

Larry was already aware of Scientology before I met him. He reckoned that where religion had failed, science could fill the gap. His view was that the mind was a vast unexplored area that we needed to know more about. I understood where he was coming from. I was after all a part-time Psychology major, when not teaching the special needs kids. I was able to attend master level courses in Psychology at St Louis University, as the Director of the school taught courses there. So rather than finishing my Bachelor's Degree in any regular fashion, I studied any course that I thought was relevant in dealing with the kids' every day needs. Now Larry was keen for me to know more about Scientology. I was reasonably happy about that. It was my hope that by finding out more about the mind and how it works, and what its capabilities were, I could in some way help the children under my care, some of whom only had a mental age of four or five, even though they were in their early teens. Without exception, they had all had a rough start to life. All sorts of disabilities were present in the children that I taught or had taught since starting at the school some six years earlier. Their problems ranged from Downs Syndrome to brain damage to autism. Most joined the school at the age of five, and would remain there until they were sixteen. My first class numbered seventeen children in the fourteen to sixteen age group, and they were all very limited academically. In spite of their limitations, I wanted to help them progress as much as I could, and was thrilled when they started to read and write. I realised as I got to know them better that they had a very uncomplicated outlook on life, with a simple faith, and a very real affection for those who helped them. As I continued at the school I taught younger children who had more academic ability. So I reasoned that the more I knew about the mind, the better equipped I would be to help those in my care.

I just hoped that the Scientology lecture that I had agreed to attend the next afternoon would be more interesting and enlightening than the book that Larry had given me to read. Called Dianetics – The Modern Science of Mental Health by L. Ron Hubbard, I had tried to get into it, partly because I was curious, and partly to please Larry, but frankly I found it very hard going – it had a boring, turgid style with a complicated message, which seemed to be presenting itself as some sort of scientific treatise. But then, I told myself, the lecture could be different again......

I was brought out of my day-dreaming by one of the kids presenting me with ten sticky glittery fingers to wash. I looked at my watch, and realised that the school day would be over in five minutes. Telling the children to come to the end of what they were doing, and begin to clear up, I started to do the same. From down the corridor the familiar sound of the school bell was heard and I dismissed the class. Tomorrow would be here in no time at all.

The next day dawned as nice as the one before. I had a deliberately lazy morning, not wanting to get into anything too complicated before the afternoon lecture. And, before I knew it, it was time to leave for our appointment with the Scientologists. After a short drive into downtown St. Louis, we arrived at a rather austere office building. Walking down a drab corridor, we found the room that we had been asked to report to. It was in fact a very functional office, with chairs and a film projector waiting to be used, a chalk board on one wall, and a couple of posters on another. The lecturer introduced himself. He was a tall, fairly good looking man, with tidy but well worn clothes, younger than I had expected, and business-like in a collar and tie.

After a few opening comments, he started to ask a few questions about us, and what brought us there. To my surprise, once he discovered that I was studying psychology, rather than being impressed he instead became openly hostile about both psychiatry and psychology. He began to lecture me about the failure of psychology and psychiatry to deal with the problem of mental illness in society and he highlighted their use of shock treatment and pre-frontal lobotomies, concentrating on their use of psychiatric drugs. As I was only a first year student of psychology I wasn't well read enough on the subject to counter his arguments. I felt my self esteem being punctured as he was so openly critical about a subject that I had given so much of my time to study.

We were then shown a video about L. Ron Hubbard, the man who had started the Scientology movement. I thought that the presentation and the video was less than intriguing, but in spite of that both Larry and I accepted the offer of a free personality test with the results being available the same day.

We were taken to another part of the building, and I hung around while Larry went through his test. Then it was my turn. I filled in a form containing around two hundred questions, and then waited to be seen by the test evaluator. In a direct and forthright way she wasted no time in analysing what I had written. She then suggested that I must be in all kinds of emotional trouble if the test results were anything to go by.

'Do you have trouble with relationships? she asked pointedly.

'Well, I suppose I do' I said, thinking briefly about my marriage break up, not realising that she had just finished the interview with my boyfriend, and therefore had more than a fair share of pertinent information about my affairs of the heart. But she picked up on my scepticism, and made no bones about the fact that my critical attitude of their organisation was a result of my being trained to think by mental health professionals and consequently my ability to make any important decision was flawed. Then she played her trump card.

'I've just enrolled Larry on the Communications Course,

and as we speak he is sitting in the course room getting started – wouldn't you like to join him? It's only going to cost you $25.00.'

I sat there, wondering how to answer. I hadn't been expecting this. But $25.00 was hardly a fortune, and it could be really helpful, I reasoned to myself – and it might be a bit of a laugh too. And anyway, I thought, it wouldn't do me any harm. If I got fed up, or too involved I could just walk away. I found myself agreeing to the suggestion, not realising for a moment the huge implications that my casual decision would have on my life. Without further ado I was taken to the course supervisor who informed me that I would be required to attend the course for a minimum of 15 hours a week. We worked out that I could probably manage that by attending three nights a week, and again on Saturday.

I was then shown the rules of the course room and some of the course materials. It was explained to me that I would need to consult a lot of dictionaries, big thick ordinary ones and special Scientology ones, as they told me that it was very important never to go past a word the meaning of which I didn't understand, as that would cloud my comprehension of what I was studying. I was then shown a curious assortment of everyday objects – erasers, small plastic toys etc, which together made up what they called a 'demo kit'. It was explained that these items were there for me to use to demonstrate the concepts I was being taught in order to show that I had understand the ideas that were being put over, a bit like an old solider over lunch would use everything on the table including the salt cellar, pepper pot and napkins to explain what happened in a particular battle using the tableware to represent other things. So for instance in order to understand the principle of two way communication you had to have these strange little objects to repre-

21

sent two people talking. I noticed that the kit which the supervisor had given me to use contained some little toy people so that made it a bit easier as I used those to show that concept. But it wasn't as easy as it might seem as you weren't allowed to talk very much about what you were trying to demonstrate as the pieces that you were moving around were meant to show what was happening. I tried to take in all that I had just agreed and had explained to me. But before I had a chance to ask any more questions, I was whisked off to start my first communication drill.

Pairing me up with my boyfriend, we were told to sit three feet apart with our eyes closed. The idea was to learn how to confront the other person and 'be there' comfortably. We were told to do this several times – sometimes for as long as half an hour on that first day. I found out later that this is the first of nine drills that are practised every day by Scientologists at every level and are used to train and drill the staff of their organisations. The result of performing this peculiar act was that I started to see lots of bright colours, and sometimes I felt as though I was watching parts of the room in bright clear light, although my eyes were tightly closed. Another result was that I became extremely light headed and quite high emotionally. In Scientology terms this is characterised as a 'win'. It's referred to as a 'win' because of the understanding that the student has now reached and from the Scientology point of view it indicates the progress they have made in reforming the thought of the person involved. I was later to discover that when one is studying communications skills, a win is when you have reached a new realization about yourself or your life and are feeling euphoric, although in reality, you're in a trancelike state.

It's difficult to explain why I didn't see through the various methods they had of getting people to accept without criticism their philosophy through the literature they produced, the 'auditing' or counselling sessions that one was required to take part in, and the long hours of study and their manipulation of the English language, because in spite of my training in psychology, and my ability to be analytical about the things I experienced and the things that happened around me, I never once made a single inquiry to anyone or to any reference book concerning L. Ron Hubbard, Dianetics, Scientology or any aspect of the organisation. And I was in a better position at that time to do so than most, having at my disposal the major reference library of a large American University as well as many professors to talk to. It seemed that I had stepped on one of those moving walkways that are so helpful in airports from getting from one area to the next. But my Scientology walkway, now that I had stepped on to it, was taking me further and further away from the reason and logic that I had had as a person all my life until this point in time. And just like a real life walkway, it was more and more difficult to turn round and go back to where I had come from. But my failure to do so was to have a huge impact on the next eight years of my life, and bring me troubles the like of which I could not yet begin to imagine. But for now, I had committed myself to the ways of the Scientologists, and I had a lot of study – and heartache – ahead of me.

Chapter Three

In At The Deep End

Although I had initially only agreed to not much more than 15 hours a week studying Scientology, it wasn't long before it began to pervade every single part of my life. I was told that I needed to keep moving forward in Scientology so that I could ultimately complete The Bridge to Total Freedom. This was not a location on a map I was told, but a path that Hubbard had laid out to show people what steps they would need to reach the high states of spiritual awareness that were available if one studied Scientology. I was informed that they were very exact steps that were laid out in a particular manner. In order to keep moving on to The Bridge one could receive counselling which they called 'auditing', but it was highly recommended that one studied the materials with a view to also becoming an auditor, so that one would be a means of others reaching these 'higher levels' too.

The training courses were described on the left hand side of a huge chart called the Grade Chart, while the auditing levels were described on the right hand side. I was soon to discover that it was a matter of tremendous importance to Scientologists to discuss and find out where you were 'on the Bridge'. If you had managed to achieve the higher levels referred to as 'Clear' and 'OT' you were held in great respect, almost as if you had magical powers! On my very first visit to the registrar, I was given a miniature copy of this chart and it was made quite clear to me that I was at a very low level of awareness and that the road to 'Total Freedom' was very clearly accessible only through Scientology training and auditing.

Only a few weeks after joining, if I was having a particularly successful evening on the course I would be sent to talk to the registrar about my next step on the Bridge to Total Freedom. The registrar could be described as a salesperson whose job it was use their persuasive powers to get their contacts to enrol on the next course. It needs to be said that they are as much victims of the system that they are working for as the people that they are in trying to enrol. Most sincerely believed that the courses they were encouraging people to get involved in would help them in their day-to-day life.

However, because of the detailed questionnaire that everyone is required to complete before starting on any of the courses, which inquires into every aspect of a person's life including past misdemeanours, bank account details and current salary levels, the Registrars were able to assess to the last penny how much money a person had at their disposal to spend on courses, and they were very skilful at lining up courses commensurate with a person's disposable income.

I personally felt more than a little overwhelmed by all the courses that were available, which all seemed to be involved in some way or other in the study of the lectures or writings of L. Ron Hubbard. I let it be known that I didn't quite know where to start and was therefore encouraged to have an interview with an auditor about my life before Scientology and what I would like to achieve from my auditing. 'Auditor' was their terminology for counsellor, someone I could in theory at least open my heart to. I was told that the courses that I was now being advised to take would be helpful to me, and would allow me ultimately to be an auditor too.

Although I guess I should have been more aware, it never struck me as odd at the time that the courses I needed to complete to become an Auditor and receive some professional auditing myself just happened to be covered – exactly – by the amount of money left in my savings account, after I had initially handed over some $3000 to them, as well as paying some of Larry's fees. This was money that my father had given to me as a gift, but as it happens he might just as well have written a cheque to the Church of Scientology for all the good it did me.

Long hours of study and evaluation meant that slowly and surely I was being dragged deeper and deeper into their net, with the result that my ability to make reasoned, balanced choices was diminished. A turning point came when I was recruited to work full time for the Scientologists. I was told that the special needs children I was currently teaching were probably that way because of their past life transgressions, and so I could better use my talents by joining their organisation, which was involved in helping the able to become more able!

Even as I wrote out my letter of resignation to the school authorities I did so with anguish in my heart. Looking back I should have heeded the warning signs, but in my eagerness to please and get involved with something that I felt was new and at the cutting edge of things, I pushed the feelings to the back of my mind, instead of treating them like the huge red light that they actually were. The truth was that I was in the process of making a massively wrong turning that would lead to years of dead-end alleys of physical, emotional and spiritual damage. I even made the decision to sell my lovely yellow BMW that David had bought for me. Boy, was I starting to make some bad moves!

I can see now that the nuns and the Monsignor who ran the school were desperate to help me, but they were too frightened by what I had become involved with, and I for my part thought that the way they were acting was because they were just very angry with me. The Monsignor even went to the point of inviting me to lunch with him in his private dining room – a rare honour – showing that he had a huge concern for me. But I made myself oblivious to this gesture of kindness.

The problem was that by this time I had been thoroughly proofed by Scientology to view anyone's criticism of the subject as a sign of their 'suppressive' anti-social tendencies and as an act on their part to try and hinder my being free to become self-determined.

Rosa, the house sister who was my classroom assistant, struggled with the fact that I was leaving. The last week was especially difficult for both of us. I would catch sight of her looking at me with tears in her eyes. Occasionally she would give me a hug and whisper 'Bonnie, won't you think again about leaving?'

The decisions that I was starting to make not only affected the folks that I worked for – it had an impact on my family too. At first I told my parents nothing about my growing interest in Scientology, and it was only when my Mom got really ill with asthma that I broached the subject at all. But as soon as my father heard me mention the name Hubbard he erupted. I found out later that Dad had read quite extensively about him in the 1950s. I didn't quite know how to handle this onslaught from my own kith and kin. But I need not have worried – the Scientologists had a answer to my problems! I was referred to an ethics officer who told me to write a letter to my dad, asking him to respect my decision as an adult to choose my way of life, which I dutifully did.

That did the trick – but the sad fact was that we hardly spoke in the ensuing years. I put him into a box in my mind labelled 'Suppressive person' and totally disconnected from him from then on. It was only after he died that I found out how much my involvement in Scientology had distressed him, and indeed the amount of anxiety it had caused the whole family. Some of my family members were scared of what I was into, others just couldn't find the right moment to say anything. It was hardly their fault, as I only got home three or four times in the long years afterwards. And as relationships between family members weren't exactly high on the Scientology agenda, it didn't trouble me after a while when I began to realise that I no longer had contact with them.

Should they have tried harder to say something? Well, Mom was great, deciding that she would remain a part of my life whether I agreed or not! She also made a point of knowing her enemy. She read all the books I gave her, and came to visit me in St. Louis. She had a real trust in the Lord, and told my grandmother, who was also a believer, that 'the generation of the upright would be blessed' and I believe that it was her 'effectual fervent prayers' and those of my grandma which caused me to come through. After all, children are given into a family by God, and no one can remove them unless He and the parent agree. I have noticed since how people in the Irish community fight for their loved ones, spending many hours talking to them, trying to warn them of the dangers that they are getting into. Sometimes it pays off, in spite of the fact that often the person has been pre-conditioned against such action.

Finally my last day at the school where I had taught for six years arrived. During my time there Mom had sewn beautiful craft aprons for me and each of the children in my class with our names embroidered on the pockets. Now on this my last day I left mine in the bottom of the box neatly folded at the back of the cupboard – an expression of what would happen to my real self during the years that I would be influenced by Scientology.

Now each evening I would go on a course at the Scientology organisation and hear of how I was shortly to become part of the team who would achieve the goals of Scientology of a 'cleared planet', when we would have a civilisation without insanity, war, crimes, etc. I had been well and truly hardened to the attempts of my friends and colleagues at St. Mary's to reach me or reason with me. Although I didn't realise it at the time I was being subjected to counselling methods that caused me to go into a euphoric, trance-like state, which in turn softened me up for the next session.

I consoled myself with the fact that I was now working for the Scientology organisation which seemed to have such high standards that they put the people connected with them through such rigorous tests. True to form I had to complete several levels of training before I was appointed to the part of the organisation responsible for bringing new people in for the lecture and personality tests. I was fairly good at recruiting people off the street, which is referred to as 'body routing'. I was taught how to approach people and who to target. My primary target was people aged between 18 and 30 who were well dressed. I was told not to approach 'degraded beings' which meant anyone who had any sort of mental or physical handicap or who looked in any way disadvantaged.

After I became proficient at body routing I had to learn how to do the test evaluation. There was a manual on how to do it, and a script. I was drilled on how to use the graph of the results. I was told to emphasise the low points on the graph as these represent problems or weaknesses, and to ignore the high points. The objective was to convince the member of the public, or 'raw meat' as they are called in Scientology, that they have huge problems, hence laying the foundation for the sale of what was to become the solution to their problems – yes, you've guessed – Scientology courses! This process is called finding the 'ruin' and then 'salvaging'.

Along with other members of staff I was given my 'stat' or statistic every week. This was a points system devised by Hubbard to measure productivity. I would get stats for every person I interviewed, and most importantly, for every person who signed up on a course. Every week my stats had to go up which meant that every week I was supposed to interview and/or sell more courses than the previous week. If I failed, I would be put onto half pay or deprived of my time off.

My next job, or 'hat' in Scientology terminology, was Registrar. I was trained in hard sell, techniques which give effect to Hubbard's directions that the public should not be given any freedom of choice or rights of privacy.

The first activity of the day around 8:30 was muster when all the staff assembled together for registration. Each staff member's name was called out by the Ethics Officer, to make sure we had turned up for work. This was also the time when any general announcements were made and when income targets were made known, which resulted in production targets being given. So, at the end of that meeting I knew how many people I needed to contact, and the level of money I would need to receive from them in order to achieve my target for the week.

Then I would go into my office and work through a list of people who had made enquiries about Scientology through reading Hubbard's book, or had given their name and phone number to a recruiter. It was reckoned by Hubbard that everyone had bought a Dianetics book was worth at least ten thousand dollars! Each book had a tear out card which people would fill in, which would give us the names and addresses that we needed.

I would then begin to work the phones, inviting people to come along to see me, and encouraging them to sign up for expensive courses, the money from which would of course go into the coffers of Scientology. Sessions with new contacts could go on for hours. In my training as Registrar I was told that people have a reactive mind and therefore can't make good choices, so part of my role was to steer them in the right direction, which meant enrolling them on more and more courses, which of course were expensive. But as a Registrar at the Church of Scientology I was paid very little – sometimes nothing at all. My hours from Monday to Friday were 8:30 a.m. until 10:30 p.m. and from 9:00 a.m. to 6:00 p.m. or 10.30 p.m. on Saturday. This was supposed to include two and a half hours of study time, but this was not always allowed. If my 'stats' were up, I would work from 9:00 a.m. till 6:00 p.m. on Sunday but if they were down I would be on cleaning duties until 10:00 p.m. Quotas always had to go up, day-by-day and week-by-week. So, if I got 20 people on a course one week, the next week I would be expected to get 25 on a course, and thirty the week after. Failure always meant punishment for what I had failed to deliver. I was earning at this point between 15 and 20 dollars a week, which was not enough to pay the rent, so I was allowed to 'moonlight' on my one day off. I found work in a Greek café working as a waitress, and I actually made more money on that one day than I did working for six days as a Registrar!

I was on staff for two and a half years between 1973 and 1976. I continued doing and paying for courses during this time. One course I tackled had not been attempted by many before or since. I'm told that it's not something that is offered anymore as some who attempted it ended up having a mental breakdown. Called The Primary Rundown it was based on the many taped lectures that Hubbard gave during his life-time. He did a particular series of lectures on the subject of study, and these lectures were considered by the Scientology hierarchy to be the most important lectures that he gave. I think there were nine lectures in total. Someone made a list of every single word he used on the tapes, on average between 8000 and 10,000 words per tape. So, on the Primary Rundown course the definition of every single word on the tape list had to be 'cleared', before the tape could be listened to, which meant that every word had to looked up in either a standard dictionary or if it was a word or phrase coined by Hubbard in a Scientology dictionary. Even small words like on, to or from which might have a dozen or more definitions each would have to be dealt with in this way, and if there were any words included in the definition that were not understood they would need to be cleared as well.

The aim of those completing this course was to achieve 'super literacy' which meant that one could grasp concepts very quickly. It took me around three or four months to complete this particular course, and the way it affected me was that I started to read material rapidly, and I found that once I came out of Scientology I had to force myself to read again at a normal rate. I not sure why the course affected me in that particular way – maybe it was because I knew there was so much I had to read, and in order to get through it all my brain started to go into overdrive almost like a car whose engine is racing too fast. I'm not absolutely sure that it was this particular course that made be react in this way, but I do know that I certainly didn't have that kind of problem before I started the course.

By the end of my first two and a half year contract with Scientology I was Director of Public Servicing. This meant that I was responsible for all of the new members of the public coming to the organisation and it was my job to oversee the test evaluations, the registrars and various events for the public.

Scientology was taking up more and more of my time, and I had let go of most of my relationships outside of their sphere. A reward for doing well on the courses, which dealt with familiarising oneself with the many words and ideas that Hubbard had written about or spoken of during his lifetime, was to be able to study more, and so Scientology began to dominate every waking moment of my life.

Larry and I had been living together for some time by now, but it was felt by some within the organisation that we were not a particularly good influence on each other, as our relationship was not helping our progress in Scientology. I was therefore instructed to move out and share an apartment with another staff member called Kate. By now Scientology's grip on my life had become strong enough for me to want to please my Auditor, and so I dutifully did as I was told. But a few months later, after Larry had completed a lot more of his counselling we got back together again, and shortly afterwards we married.

My first staff contract expired in November 1976. By now however I seemed to be on a fast track as far as Scientology was concerned. I learned quickly and easily. And although Larry was the one that initially introduced me to Scientology his progress did not match mine. It wasn't entirely his fault. A job I was to be offered included massive amounts of auditing and course work as part payment, causing me to leap way ahead of him.

On one of my more successful body routing sessions I had recruited an extremely wealthy businessman to Scientology called Charles, who, together with his wife Anne_, totally embraced the Scientology teachings. One day some time later as I was just about to get down to some course work of my own he rang me with a proposal I found hard to refuse.

'Hi Bonnie – how are you?', Charles said, his distinct drawl being instantly recognisable. He wasted no time in telling me why he was phoning.

'Anne and I have been talking about the way forward for ourselves, now that we have come into Scientology and with our first child due shortly, and we were wondering if once the child arrives you would consider becoming our nanny? Obviously it would have to be a live-in appointment, but Larry could come with you of course! We'd be so grateful if you could consider it. And in order to help you with your own Scientology study, we would like to buy some auditing and course work for you, as part of your employment package. Talk it through with Larry and let us know what you think.'

To be honest, Larry wasn't crazy about the idea from the word go, but the deal appealed to me – Charles had a fabulous house, just the kind of place that I could get accustomed to! And the auditing would be a help in getting me further along on the Scientology road. So I agreed to take up the post of nanny, and Charles paid for the courses that I would eventually go on.

Then after about a year I was approached by another Scientologist, Bonnie Bishop, to set up an 'Apple' School in St Louis. She had attended a meeting which had been called by Scientology parents who wanted some kind of private education for their children, based on Scientology teaching. I went along with Charles and his wife and after the meeting when Bonnie and I were talking she discovered that my background was in education. She later wrote to the parents saying she was willing to start an Apple school in the area, as long as I was in charge! This was quite a feather in my cap. I was learning fast, and each new ladder that was put in front of me I was eager to climb. It also suited my situation. Although I loved the house I was living in, and the baby was cute, there were also drawbacks which I hadn't known about when taking up the post. Anne was writing a book, and I discovered that along with my work with the baby, I was expected to do a certain amount of editing of her book also, which in the end just got too much for me to cope with. So I left Charles employment and although I left on good terms with him and his wife, my marriage with Larry was not so cordial. In fact it was all but over.

I set about my new job at the Apple school with enthusiasm. Scientology was the basis of every lesson, and so just like any adult on a Scientology course, each child was given a Scientology dictionary as well as an ordinary one, in order that they could fully understand or 'clear' every word of the lesson that was before them. So for instance, in a maths lesson it could be weeks before a child would get on to simple arithmetic, as all words in their text books had to be 'cleared' by the child before any calculations could commence. And as they were working through the words in their maths book they could be required to use their demo kit to illustrate how much understanding they were gaining from the words that were being studied. So, to take the maths lesson as an example, lets say that one of the words on the Arithmetic check sheet was multiplication. The child would have to move the pieces of the demo kit around in such a fashion that his study partner or 'twin' could see the concept of multiplying something in the way that he moved the pieces around. And this procedure would go on throughout all the subjects that were being studied. Even sport subjects like football did not escape the need to 'clear' words and the emphasis that Hubbard put on drills, where a child was expected to repeat the same action over and over again until they had perfected it. One kind of Drill is called 'Chinese School' where the children sit as a group and repeat important facts together, over and over again. So in the case of football the supervisor would 'Chinese School' the rules until they were known very well.

Apple School started to take children from the age of five, and some would teach kids up to high school level. But each school was different. My school had a core group of about twenty children from Scientology families, but the rest were made up of children who were drop outs from the normal school system. Life is always better understood in hindsight, and I now believe I was trying to console myself that I was happy in Scientology by returning to the job that I loved the most, which was teaching.

With the help of some of the parents we renovated two dilapidated store front buildings after which the school grew to about fifty students. I was then asked to help oversee another new Apple School that had started in Kansas City, Missouri, and another in Michigan and a third in Minneapolis! So I became the Midwest Director of Apple Schools. Life seemed to take a turn for the better and I was able to feel once again that children were genuinely being helped.

Charles eventually bought a school building for us to move into, which had far better facilities than our original storefront school. After my success at the St Louis school I started ones in other parts of America including Kansas City and Detroit.

The Apple Schools became one of the front groups for Scientology. Although they used Hubbard's study technology the link with Scientology was never clearly declared to parents making inquiries. In February 1977 after I had set up the school, I went to Los Angeles to do some of the advanced courses that Charles had paid for some time back, in order that I could continue to progress 'up the Bridge'. By now I was way ahead of Larry, and that, coupled with the fact that he didn't like living in our new surroundings even though they were luxurious beyond my wildest dreams were the main reasons why our marriage started to fall apart and ultimately fail completely.

In June 1977 I reached the state of 'Clear'. Very soon after reaching this state I completed the first three Operating Thetan levels. The materials for the Operating Thetan levels are kept highly confidential by the Church of Scientology. The reason the Scientology organisation gave for keeping these Operating Thetan or 'OT' levels so secret was because if a person saw them before they had been prepared by going through all the other different levels first, the power of the knowledge they contained could cause them to contact a dreadful disease or even die! When a person comes on to the OT levels, the idea that they are not themselves but a composite of disembodied spirits that were jammed together so many trillion years ago is introduced. It really did start to get quite demonic. The student in a very subtle way is being introduced to dabbling in artificial schizophrenia, as they are encouraged to speak to the spirits which they are told make up their body, mind and personality. When I look back on these courses now I feel that I was horribly deceived. I can now see that the contents of the OT3 materials are far removed from Hubbard's claims that Scientology and Dianetics were scientifically tested methods towards self improvement. However, by the time I completed the OTIII level, my powers of critical thought had been eroded to such an extent that I was unable to see this at the time. I then went on to complete the next two OT levels.

By now, as a Grade IV Class IV auditor, and an 'OT III', I was quite an advanced Scientologist! I returned to St. Louis where I became the Executive Director of the Apple School in St. Louis. And I was to go further up the ladder before I went into a huge spiral which turned out to be part of God's escape plan for me.

NB: Before continuing to read the rest of my story, I recommend at this point that you take a break and turn to the end of the book to read Appendix One, What the Scientologists Don't Tell You. As you will probably have realised by now, the theories and structures of the Church of Scientology are complex and completely alien to the ways most of us live our lives. It is difficult to explain, solely through my own experiences, how Scientology came into being and exactly what its followers believe, so I have written this factual appendix based on the published works of Jon Atack, who has conducted extensive research into the history of Scientology and its founder, L. Ron Hubbard, over many years.

Chapter Four

Light At The End Of The Tunnel

All the studying, auditing and career responsibilities that now made up my life didn't leave much time for social interaction. And by now virtually all the people that touched my life were connected with Scientology in one way or another. Some time after I divorced Larry I bumped into someone from my early days in Scientology, a man called Bob. About 5'9" tall, he was very thin with sandy brown hair, and spoke with a quiet authority. He had worked for years as Scientology's Public Relations Director and was now a highly trained Scientologist who had specialist instruction in how to deal with the press and officials who had questions about the organisation. He had studied to be a teacher but had become a Scientology staff member in the early 1970s'.

I had first come into contact with him years before when he was the Communications Course Supervisor on the first Scientology course I went on. We lost touch when he went away to do more training in California, about the time I separated from Larry he came back from California though only briefly before returning once again.

Then when Charles paid for me to have some training in California, I met up with Bob again. In Scientology terms he was a good catch. By this time I lost any meaningful relationship with my natural family, apart from Mom and my grandmother, and with two broken relationships behind me I longed for a bit of stability, and the chance to be a mother myself. Marriage to Bob seemed to offer all of those things. Within a short space of time I had agreed to marry him.

It seems significant looking back that we were married at sunrise on July 8th and the first telegram we received was not one of congratulations but of the news that the Scientology headquarters in Los Angeles had been raided by officials of the Federal Government. Bob spent the rest of our wedding day and many to follow writing press releases from his office.

We moved into the upstairs flat above the shop front building that housed the Apple School. Now I wanted what neither David nor Larry had been able to give me – a child of my own. The ability to become pregnant seemed to elude me again now that I was married to Bob, so in the end I persuaded him to consider the possibility of us becoming foster parents. But when we started to talk to the official we had to see, having filled in the necessary forms, she started to tell us that she also had details of children who needed to be adopted. This put the whole conversation into a different gear, and the end result of our discussion was that we were able to adopt an adorable nine-month-old girl with beautiful blond hair and deep blue eyes, who we called Desiree.

When news came through that she was ready for collection Bob was away getting more training in L.A. He obviously wanted to come home at that point, but his superiors were unwilling to let him. This started to put a terrific strain on our marriage. In the end he did come home a week after she arrived, without permission, but he was disciplined heavily for that. That was probably the point when Scientology started to keep a file on me, and my growing disaffection with their authoritarian control. Of course I didn't know that at the time, and I'm not sure that I would have cared too much either. I was just so happy to be responsible for this wonderful little person who had come into our lives, and I couldn't wait to get all my daily work completed, so that I could spend some time with her.

My personal life now seemed to be on a more even keel, and things also seemed to be working out just fine at the Apple School in St Louis. Pupils, parents and staff all appeared to be happy, and ten per cent of all that we were making was being sent to Scientology Headquarters, which meant that they were happy too.

Charles had by this point purchased a huge school building for us, which was great after struggling with the original storefront building. The new building originally housed an elementary school which had stopped functioning. It was a remarkable facility, but we couldn't begin to meet the cost of running it with only 45 fee-paying children.

But during the first few months of the school being opened, however, I met a team of artists called On the Wall Productions who created individual murals with the help of children and so we designed a mural project that stretched the entire length of the walls on the outside of the building. This generated a lot of publicity for the school and for a while I was flavour of the month with the Guardians Office where Bob worked.

Then one day news reached me that one of the personnel from the main Apple school in Los Angeles who had been responsible for creating the curriculum and all the materials that we used, had got into ethics trouble with the Guardians Office – an important branch of Scientology administration. The problem was that he had started to question some of the material that Hubbard had written, which was bad enough in itself, but then he had written some teaching material himself, which was contrary to Hubbard's teaching, which he distributed to the Apple Schools for their use. As a result of these actions he was declared to be a Suppressive person. This had enormous repercussions. Each Apple school in the network of schools across the country was visited by Guardians Office personnel and we were told that we needed to destroy all the materials we were using that this guy had written and that they were there to observe that we complied with this order! I couldn't help being reminded of some of the incidents mentioned in George Orwell's famous book 1984! I was very much opposed to the destruction of the material, and made my thoughts known to both Bonnie Bishop and the staff members of my school. This normally would not have been a smart move as my staff were duty bound to report any dissenting remarks to the Guardians office. Bonnie Bishop however didn't like the instruction that we had received to destroy some much teaching material any more than I did, and started to make steps to stop some of the money that the Apple Schools were paying each month to Scientology Headquarters. It would be an understatement to say this didn't go down very well with them, and her actions started an investigation by the Guardians Office into all the Apple Schools.

At this point both Bonnie Bishop and I were looked upon with great suspicion, so a few months later when I hurt my back whilst playing sport, I shouldn't have been surprised that I was promptly removed from my post. I was informed by an official from the security division of the Church that I could not go back to my post until I had been to L.A. for some auditing. This was out of my reach financially, so the upshot was that I was not allowed to go back to the school to work even when I recovered from my back problem.

The auditing that I had been ordered to receive by the Guardian's office was connected with the secret OT levels that I had previously completed. The trouble was that OT's who lived outside of Los Angeles and Clearwater Florida were not allowed to receive any auditing in the lower level organisations that exist in most of the other major cities of America. I was told to find the money to return to the Advanced Organisation in Los Angeles. The treatment they meted out to me had a lot to do with my vociferous opposition to their "book burning" edicts, but my back injury became a convenient hook to hang my dismissal on. There was no point in trying to make them rethink their decision. I knew that once such a verdict had been given it would not be reversed.

In spite of this career setback, I still seemed destined to become more deeply involved with Scientology as time went by. And it was to come about by another division of the Scientology movement called the Sea Organisation, more commonly called The Sea Org. It's an administration department within the Church of Scientology whose purpose is to ensure compliance and conformity with Hubbard's scriptures. It has to be said that it is considered by many within Scientology to be an elite organisation, and holds a certain amount of street cred, to all those within the Scientology movement who have not reached those dizzy heights.

It was not unusual for recruiters from the Sea Organisation in Los Angeles to visit the outer organisations located in the other states of America. They went on missions with a view to interviewing 'public' Scientologists to see if they would come to work and live communally in Los Angeles. And sure enough, one of their number looked me up. The woman who contacted me was called Barbara. She had asked me to make an appointment to see her at her office, and as she shuffled through some papers on her untidy desk I had time to observe the woman who sat before me. She was very small in stature, with dark neat hair, cut in a severe, businesslike style, wearing navy blue tailored uniform. Her manner was dedicated and determined.

'Bonnie, I know you'll appreciate it if I tell you immediately why I wanted to see you', she said, looking at me with unblinking eyes, no doubt trying to gauge what my reaction might be to what she was about to say.

'I've been looking at your files, and I think the skills you have as a teacher would be of great value in one of our main headquarters of Scientology in L.A. We're looking for someone to restructure the educational facility for the children of Sea Org members, called The Cadet Organisation. I have no doubt that you would be the ideal person to create a great school for the children. And Bob could be really used too. He tells me that he really wants to be a highly trained auditor, and I've already offered him the opportunity to supervise the Class 8 training level. Now I'm making you an offer Bonnie. I'd like you to think about it seriously.'

I discovered that Bob was as excited about the new opportunity he had been offered as I was about mine. But everything was not as cut and dried as it looked at first glance. We were still in debt to Charles for the money that he had paid for me to complete my OT levels, which was now my financial responsibility as I was no longer working for him. But when I mentioned this to Barbara she persuaded Charles to cancel my debt and consider it a donation to the Sea Organisation, telling him that it was an admirable thing for him to do to further the goals of Scientology. After that was agreed it didn't take me long to accept her offer.

Bob and I then sold everything we owned to pay off the assorted debts we had and packed a few personal belongings into a pickup truck that he had hired to drive to San Francisco.

At the time I was flattered to be recruited by The Sea Org, who obviously wanted to use my teaching skills as much as possible, but in hindsight it was a very regrettable day in January 1981 when I joined them at the American Saint Hill Organisation (shortened to ASHO) in Los Angeles, and pledged to subscribe to their goals and purposes for the next billion years! For those thinking that signing up to anything for that length of time is bizarre, it does have its own logic, however strange it might appear to outsiders. Scientologists are told that when they die – or 'drop the body' they are then free to pick up another body, and in that way are able to continue working for millions of years!

Although in Scientology terms it was a big step up to become involved with the Sea Org, it was in fact personally the beginning of a huge downward spiral. We moved to the communal housing for staff in Los Angeles which turned out to be a derelict Hollywood Inn right across the road from the famous Grauman's Chinese Theatre, not that I ever saw any movie- stars or movies for that matter!

If I was excited at becoming a member of the Sea Org. it was short lived and unwarranted. Living conditions were appalling and life was pretty grim. Our room was on the seventh floor, the elevators weren't working and we were given a double room with a bathroom adjoining. The only view was a window to the back of the hotel over what appeared to be a garbage heap running down the centre of the hotel.

If life was grim, the schedule was equally gruelling. We worked from around 8:30 a.m. to 10:30 p.m. with a two hour break from five in the evening which was called 'family time'. The real tragedy was that not only had we committed ourselves to this dreadful regime, but it also affected Desiree who by this time was three years old.

Desi was taken care of daily in the Sea Org nursery and conditions were deplorable there. If I was allowed my 'family time' – and once or twice a week I was not – I would walk the two miles or so to the nursery to collect Desi and take her back with us to ASHO for dinner between 6 pm. to 7 p.m. After dinner we had to take her back to the nursery or to a babysitting unit we had managed to get set up at Fountain Building before starting work or study again at 7 p.m.

I was allowed to spend less and less time with my little girl and I got increasingly upset. She was at the nursery for many hours where the conditions were appalling. The furniture was old and dangerous, the staff unqualified, and there was no proper equipment or toys for the children to play with. There was no garden to play in, just a bare yard with sand on the ground, and I found it very upsetting that I had so little time with her, and the conditions worried me. Obviously the levels that I had been through had not cleared me of all critical thinking because my thoughts were far from harmonious towards the Sea Org. management for the way Bob and I and our little girl were being treated.

I started to tell Bob how I was feeling, but rather than offering the support that I needed, he reported me to the Ethics Officer who decided that I should be disciplined. As part of my daily routine I was given the menial job of lugging files around from the Central Registry Files. I was shocked that my husband would report me for speaking my mind in private, but I should have known better. It is in fact consistent with Scientology policy. The Church of Scientology demands conformity and obedience from all its members. It will not tolerate dissent from within or without the organisation. It disciplines those members who do anything which the Church disapproves of. It enforces internal discipline through the system devised by Hubbard known as 'ethics'. And it is an 'ethics offence' to contravene Hubbard's policies! Scientologists who become aware of such contraventions are obliged to report them to an Ethics Officer, hence the action taken by Bob against me.

As I said, my assignment was lugging heavy files around, but it might have been a reduction in salary, deprivation of leisure time or a reduction in rations. Repeated and serious offences can lead to expulsion for the Church and declaration as a 'suppressive person'.

You need to understand that in the Sea Org. in particular, ethics is all encompassing. It is used to control every aspect of ones'life, even relationships with other people. Every staff and Sea Org. member effectively becomes an informant. If you fail to report a 'crime' then you are guilty of the crime yourself! Crimes against Scientology are called 'suppressive acts' and Hubbard defined these as 'actions or omissions undertaken to knowingly suppress, reduce or impede Scientology or Scientologists'. Hubbard provided a list of suppressive acts in a policy letter written in December 1965. This list includes such things as 'public disavowal of Scientology', 'public statements against Scientology' and 'intentional and unauthorised alteration of technology, policy, issues or check sheets'.

The Church is just as mean minded towards organisations or individuals not part of the Church who oppose them. True to form, Hubbard produced a number of policy letters on how to deal with critics of Scientology. The basic position is to attack, never defend. As Hubbard said in a letter dated 25th February 1966 'Make it rough, rough on the attackers all the way. The other advice that he gave was as follows:

Spot who is attacking us

Start investigating them promptly for Felonies or worse, using our own professionals, not outside agencies.

Double curve our reply by saying we welcome an investigation of them.

Start feeding lurid, blood, sex crimes, actual evidence on the attackers to the press.

Similar advice, in a letter dated 15th August 1960, on how to respond to a threat was to 'make enough threat or clamour to cause the enemy to quail..... if attacked on some vulnerable point ...... always find or manufacture enough threat against them to cause them to sue for peace... always attack'.

I began to realise that I was trapped in a marriage and a lifestyle that was dictated by their rules and regulations. I kept trying to comfort myself with the idea that as soon as I had finished my basic training I would be allowed to take over the children's facilities and really make a difference for Desi and the other children. The Sea Org is run according to naval regulations and rules, and according to Hubbard's teaching, the needs and goals of the group must take precedence over the needs of the individual or any family unit, so it was ultimately decided that I would be better utilised as a Sea Org. recruiter than a teacher.

What started to happen to me was that my whole personality, as well as my principles, goals and dreams were being reconstructed into a person I can now hardly recognise as myself. All the things I had previously thought to be valuable and vital were discarded and I became a dedicated staff member and a somewhat heartless human being.

But hidden somewhere in my heart, and protected from the tentacles of Hubbard's mindset was a voice that kept crying out for me to listen. So, after a year I began to tell Bob that I wanted to go – to get out of the organisation and its rules and regulations and its total control. He said if I ever left it would be without him. I thought over what he said, then pride got in the way, as I began to speculate on what my parents would think about another failed marriage, as well as time and money wasted in Scientology.

In spite of all this however I approached the Ethics Officer to say that I seriously doubted whether I could continue. The reaction I got was not at all what I had expected.

'Bonnie, we value you as a member, but I can see you need to get some time to yourself. I'm going to give you permission to take time out – three days to be precise. Go and have a wander around. It'll help you remember what it was like before you found Scientology. Then report to me at the end of that time. I'll let Bob know what you are doing.'

The next three days turned out to be a totally surreal experience as I sat on a myriad of park benches in downtown Hollywood watching the street people go about their business, trying to work out how.they survived. Although I was technically free to wander where I wanted to, I had very little money on me, and had to return home to sleep every night. My 'freedom' therefore was probably no more than a five mile radius with heavy financial restrictions on what I could actually do.

After my three days of freedom I reported once more to the Ethics Officer who assigned a series of actions to help me work out my destiny. Called Conditions Formulas they are assigned to a staff member to describe the condition they are in as far as their relationship to the group goes. The lowest or worst condition that one can be in is 'Confusion', followed by Treason, Enemy, Doubt, and Liability before one comes into the slightly higher conditions of Non-Existence, Danger, Emergency, Normal, Affluence and then the highest conditions of Power Change and Power. The conditions lower than 'Doubt' reflect the actions of the staff member towards the group that are dangerous for the group, the names of the conditions reflecting the degree of the danger. Each condition had certain steps to follow and when those under review believe that they have completed the step in question they are required to write up why they believed they have finished that condition and what they had done to prove that they had. They then had to ask permission of the Ethics Officer to be upgraded to the next Higher Condition. Once the condition of Liability is reached they then have to decide on a project that would win the approval of the group again before petitioning each member to be allowed to rejoin the group. Just admitting wanting to leave the Sea Org gave me an automatic assignment of 'the condition of doubt' to the group.

During the time these conditions are being worked through one is made to do amends projects like cleaning toilets or other menial tasks. The person under review is removed from their post during this time and is viewed by the others as not to be trusted with any real responsibility. The person's progress is recorded on a chart. A continuingly low trend on the graph might result in the assignment of a lower condition as it would be looked upon as a betrayal of the group as a whole. I went through the whole demeaning process, and was finally accepted once more by my group.

As a reward for my recanting my doubts I was given the position of Director of Processing (Counselling) and was put in charge of taking care of all the 'public' Scientologists who had paid a great deal of money to purchase their 'spiritual freedom'. It was now my job to make sure that auditors under my control were operating productively which meant ensuring that lots of people who had paid for their auditing hours completed the programs which then allowed them to take the next step on The Bridge. So it was be necessary for instance to make sure that the people who had paid for the services of an auditor would be scheduled to arrive on time and ready to go into session with their auditor.

To an already gruelling schedule was added the responsibility of seeing that the public Scientologists who had booked time for counselling received their next step on the 'Bridge'. The regime began to take its toll on my health. The conditions Bob, Desiree and I lived under were close to those of a concentration camp. One of the disciplinary measures that was used at the time was control of our diet. What we ate, how much free time we were allowed, and how long our duties lasted each day, were based on our weekly production targets being met. The overall statistic that was of the greatest concern to management was the gross income. If the amount of money the organisation produced weekly was not ever increasing then certain disciplinary actions were taken. At this time we were being fed rice and beans three times a day. And 'Liberty Time', which had amounted to one day off a week had been cancelled.

The days seemed to disappear one after the other with hardly a distinguishing point between them. It wasn't unusual at the end of the day for the entire 'crew' to be assigned to 'renovations' duty which required us to assist in physically renovating the hospital buildings which Scientology had purchased for its headquarters.

I am sure you must be wondering why I didn't leave if things were so bad. Well, it's almost impossible to describe the level of physical and mental fatigue I was experiencing at that in time. Having been reformed in my thinking about wanting to leave, I seemed to slip into some automatic mode where I simply moved through each day with as little questioning as about why I was submitting to such a way of life as possible. One is also taught to believe that the individual must be ultimately, completely, responsible for their 'condition' in Scientology. It's a guilt inducing system and the technology of Scientology is considered to be flawless.

Christmas Day that year was very sad. As we often received as little as $15.00 a week, there was precious little money for any gifts. I watched Desiree scrambling up and down the long hallway, playing with her few dolls as I sat at my huge wooden desk at one end. I was required to be 'on post' as I had not managed to keep the 'auditing' hours increasing from one week to the next in the weeks prior to Christmas week.

Then halfway through the afternoon, I was astonished to see a tall, very tastefully dressed, and extremely handsome man approach me carrying a bottle of champagne and two delicate flutes! I half-remembered my English friend Geoffrey mentioning some conversations that he had had with his roommate, another Englishman by the name of Richard, and asking if I could spare the time to help him. As I thought the world of Geoff ever since we had done some of the upper secret levels of Scientology together in Hollywood and he had always been so kind to me, I had agreed to meet Richard.

It was very peculiar meeting him, as I had this feeling that he would become a very important part of my life. It was something like a Jonathon/David story that is recorded in the Bible – the recognition that here is someone you've only just met that you know for certainty will change your entire life. Because of course I had no way of knowing that this tall, handsome Englishman who at that point had enough time on a Christmas afternoon to find out more about Scientology, would one day lead me out of the living nightmare I was in. I had no way of knowing that a new adventure was about to begin. He had arrived not a moment too soon.

But how, you may be wondering, did he get to the point where he was looking for answers to life in a Scientology office on a Christmas afternoon? Well, why don't I let him tell you that himself in the next chapter..........

Chapter Five

Richard's Story – In His Own Words

Before I tell you how I came to be with Geoff on that memorable Christmas Day, I need to take you back a few years to the Christmas of 1977 when I, together with Elizabeth, the woman I was married to then, and our new son Benjamin, were enjoying a holiday in the Channel Islands in the home of Elizabeth's uncle which made a pleasant change from our home town of Worthing. He'd also invited Liz's cousin Valerie and her husband Frank who had travelled from sunny California to spend Christmas with us all.

We all got on well, and during the course of the Christmas break they asked if we would like to spend the following Christmas with them in Beverly Hills. The idea really appealed. Elizabeth was a struggling actress, and California was at the heart of the American movie industry. As for me, the thought of living in a warm climate sounded idyllic. The more we talked about it in the ensuing months the more we thought – why just settle for Christmas – why not go and live there? So, instead of planning a Christmas break, we mentally changed gear and started to make plans to sell our house and everything that we owned to begin a new life in America.

By the time Christmas 1978 rolled round we were in

Beverly Hills, sharing a house with Valerie and Frank, certainly nothing that we had originally thought about when Elizabeth and I had married in 1971, and a world away from our life on the south coast of England.

My childhood in Worthing had been fairly standard. I grew up with my elder brother John and our mum and dad. Dad worked for the local Council so although we were never short of money, it wasn't in abundant supply either.

I managed to get through childhood and school without any major scrapes or mishaps, not shining in any one subject particularly, but I really enjoyed sport. In fact I represented my school at some time or other in virtually every sport, as well as representing the County schools at football. But eventually the day came when I finally left my studies behind, and tried my hand at several jobs until I found my niche as a salesman for a car dealership in Worthing.

For the first few months we were in America we lived with my cousin-in-law and her husband in Beverly Hills. The house they were renting overlooked what is known as The Flats of Beverly Hills. It was luxuriously appointed, with its own swimming pool – a far cry from anything I had experienced before. But even better things were to come. The place overlooking the flats was somewhere they had rented while their new house in Coldwater Canyon was being built. As soon it was completed we all moved in. It was quite a location to move to. If the rented house could be described as extremely comfortable, then this was palatial, and included sauna, a pool with a canyon top view, tennis courts and 40 foot mature palm trees, planted the week before we took possession.

Our road was not without its celebrities. Charlton Heston lived on one side of the street and Burt Bacharach lived on the other, which at the time for us was quite a bizarre experience. The whole neighbourhood seemed to be caught up in the tennis courts/sauna/swimming pool circuit, which was one tough lifestyle – but someone had to live it!

It took a week or two to adjust to all the changes that we were encountering, but even so, within six weeks I had found a huge vacant building and fitted it out to house a cabinet making company, deciding to try my hand at customised cabinet making, a vast industry in America at the time. Within eight weeks and with financial backing from a bank, together with all the money we had brought with us from England I rented a workplace, bought machinery and hired staff. Ahmed was my employee, an Arab originally from Egypt and although he was working for me he was also to become a good friend. Around this time Elizabeth, Ben and I moved into a house of our own, in Sherman Oaks, in the San Fernando Valley area of Los Angeles.

It seemed only a few months later, when I had started to get busy, that news of my father's death came through, via my brother John. I had known for some time that Dad had not been well, but the news was still devastating. Dad's health was one of several things I had to consider when deciding to go and live in America. He had been diagnosed as having cancer a while before our move. I talked over our idea with him, and he insisted that we take the chance that was there for us.

Years later, Mum gave me a small tattered and well thumbed Bible that I had originally been given by the Salvation Army when from the age of 5 to 9 I attended a Sunday School run by them. Mum told me Dad carried it everywhere with him when he did his job with the Council visiting elderly people in their homes to estimate maintenance repairs, etc. This came as a surprise, because I didn't know he held any Christian beliefs. But maybe the things that he experienced in a Prisoner Of War hospital during World War Two had moved him in that direction.

I travelled to England on my own for the funeral, spent a few days with Mum and John, before returning once again to the USA. Once back I put all my energy into the business and it prospered for a while, but after a spate of working incredibly long hours the demand started to dry up. Within two years the business had floundered. When Ahmed started to realise what was happening to the business he told me that he would go home and pray about it. I asked who he would be praying to because as far as I was concerned there was no one there and he replied that he prayed to the foreman, Jesus, to ask the Boss on my behalf!

Sadly my business was not the only thing to hit the rocks. Following its collapse came the end of my marriage to Liz. She felt that I was going nowhere in this land where success is everything, and filed for divorce, moving out and taking Ben with her.

I also had to vacate the house we shared and because I couldn't afford to provide maintenance Liz moved into an apartment which I guess was funded by her cousin. I found what I called 'a hole in the wall' apartment and after a few weeks of basic living – my daily diet was a can of baked beans – and a lot of help and financial assistance from newly found friends I secured employment, again in the motor trade selling Mercedes in downtown L.A., which was a pretty hair-raising job. I'm not sure how, but I seemed to have a natural aptitude to sell – I was selling copy paper in Sweden by the time I was 20, and eventually became a very young manager of the Mercedes Benz dealership in Worthing. My problem was that I rarely found an ethical product made by an ethical company. Sadly, my Mercedes job didn't really work out, so I got employment with an East Coast company representing a floral line of goods over the entire state of California. This lasted as long as it took for me to establish new accounts and for the company to split my territory into a quarter of the size – something that I had had a major hand in organising.

In all of the time I had spent in California I had always somehow kept up my love of the game of squash and spent many hours playing in a club which was run by an Englishman a hours' drive away from where I lived. This squash club was a home away from home for all kinds of international squash players and I played the game with a passion, having been in the Sussex Squash league for Brighton's 5th team before moving to the States.

During this period of continual change I became very good friends with Geoffrey, another exile from the UK. He had spent a lot of his life working in Canada before arriving in L.A. He quickly became a dear friend but what I didn't know then was that for a very long time he had been a Scientologist. And on one of a number of frequent visits to his apartment when we would get together to play backgammon with another English friend of his, who was also a Scientologist, he introduced me to the sub-study of Scientology called Dianetics.

This came about because I began to share some of the problems of my recent past and how upset I felt. After a usual friendly evening of backgammon he started what became a familiar routine known to me as Dianetic counselling, or auditing as it is called by Scientology. This he did by asking me to relax, even to shut my eyes if it helped – which did help, and he very sensitively asked me to recount the circumstances which were plaguing me and giving me such emotional concern.

This was the start of several informal sessions and very quickly I realised that I was looking forward to the experience; I felt strangely mellow after each counselling session – almost carefree – light headed even. He gave me several books written by the founder of Dianetics and Scientology, L. Ron Hubbard. I read them voraciously. However it didn't appear to be too long before he became almost disturbed by the now constant demand I was placing on him and his ability to counsel me in this particular way. He suggested that he couldn't help me any more and that he was going to introduce me to a friend of his who worked for the Scientology Organisation just six blocks from where his apartment was. I couldn't quite believe it when he suggested that we go on Christmas Day of all days to see her. But then I didn't have much else to do, and if his friend could help well, maybe it would be all worth it. He told me that his friend's name was Bonnie......

Following a rushed Christmas Day meal, we drove to the Scientology Headquarters in downtown Los Angeles. They turned out to be in a large rectangular shape building, probably built around the early 1940's and originally housing the famous Cedars of Lebanon hospital. It was known by Scientology members as the 'blue building' because of the light powder blue exterior colour, which gave off a rather dingy appearance. It's official front entrance, which is shown on most publicity shots, bearing at it's pinnacle the Scientology cross, never actually seems to be used. Like everyone else we used the lesser Berendo Street access at the side of the building.

The lifts were not working, a phenomena that I was to get used to as I visited on subsequent occasions, so we walked up several flights of stairs before turning into a long and badly lit corridor. As I walked along this corridor with

Geoffrey I saw a petite woman dressed in patchwork denim jeans and matching top. She had a sunny disposition and a lovely warm smile. Geoffrey stopped in front of her and said to me 'Richard, this is Bonnie.' I was carrying a bottle of Moet and Chandon and two crystal flutes especially for the occasion aiming to impress her, yet felt strangely sad that she had to work on what was considered by the rest of the western world to be a national holiday. Nevertheless I was very keen to seek her help as she came with such recommendation from Geoffrey. After politely excusing himself Geoffrey left us together.

Bonnie was very skilful at putting me at ease and I quickly began to relate my problems to her. The rest of the day just flew by and although Bonnie was supposed to be working on other projects she somehow managed to spend most of it with me! I couldn't possibly have realised how much this almost fateful day was going to help mould and form the rest of my life. Bonnie's cheeky smile and sparkling eyes captivated me and in no time at all it seemed that I was only at peace when I was in her company.

There was something about her that I really clicked with, and neither of us had to try hard to get on with each other. I was eager to get any counselling that she could give me. The brief 'highs' that I had experienced from Geoffrey's counselling had already begun to create a craving in me to continue at all costs. Bonnie and I quickly became good friends, and I found myself making any old excuse to see her. As often as the organisation allowed I took her away from the obviously gruelling schedule she was working under, and out to dinner. I have to be honest and say that I partially wanted to spend time with her as a person in her own right, but I also wanted to receive as much counselling from her as I could as she was very skilled at her work. I saw in her eyes a radiant light, and before I knew it I was falling in love with her. I had found in her my first really true friend who I felt inexorably drawn to, not being able to help myself in my blatant and overt moves to be with her as often as I could.

But something was wrong, and I couldn't at first figure out what it was. She kept her own feelings very much to herself, but in an off- guarded moment she admitted to me one evening that she was not feeling well. I was immediately concerned, and suggested that she seek medical help, but she seemed curiously reluctant to do that. Each time I suggested that was what she ought to be doing she very firmly but definitely brushed off the idea, even though I now knew that she was in pain most of the time. I thought that perhaps she had a fear of doctors, and then thought that maybe she had some kind of terminal cancer. What I failed to realise was that the relentless physical pain and discomfort she was experiencing was compounded by the mental anguish she was going through in having to stay 'on post' as Hubbard had dictated in internal policy letters, and not allow her 'case', as they referred to her medical condition, to detract her from the more important work of the Organisation.

Things however came to a head one evening when Bonnie called Geoffrey because she was feeling very unwell and had had to leave work. Geoffrey, who knew what she had been going through physically as much as I did, took decisive action and literally moved her out of her commune lodgings opposite the blue building and into his apartment close by, after having a few choice words with Bob, telling him that he thought he had screwed up the whole idea of taking care of her and so he would be taking over Bonnie's care from now on. What he said was not without substance

– even the accommodation that Bob and Bonnie lived in was gross – one squalid, sparsely furnished room, together with a kitchen that didn't have cooking appliances and a bathroom with gaping holes in the walls.

Geoff called me and told me what he had done, and I then rang to see how she was. It was obvious as I spoke to her that she needed rest and was in a great deal of pain and discomfort. Circumstances had rendered me incapable of doing much to help. I couldn't offer any financial help, and I was living many miles away at a friend's house, so couldn't even pay her a visit.

Meanwhile the Scientology organisation were under orders to 'recover' her and get her back into their confines, but Geoff and I made a stand and kept them from hounding her personally. They didn't give up without a struggle, and were determined that they would get her. They tried several times, knocking on Geoffrey's apartment door in full pseudo-navel uniform demanding her return but Geoff and I were equally determined that this was not going to happen. As it transpired they didn't have any medical insurance cover for their members and Bonnie, like the majority of staff members of Scientology ,had no financial means to pay for any medical help. Effectively she was penniless and without medical cover. In America it's not that simple if you need medical attention and live under those kind of circumstances. There is a poor system called Medicaid but the form filling and acceptance procedures take a long time to complete. Geoffrey had put these in motion on Bonnie's behalf and was waiting for a response, but time ran out and the pain Bonnie was now getting became overwhelming. Geoffrey immediately paid whatever he could in lieu of Medicaid acceptance and took Bonnie to the hospital where she underwent immediate major surgery.

The surgery she needed was abdominal and her condition was serious. As it happened the doctor who operated on Bonnie was an eminent surgeon who specialised in Obstetrics and Gynaecology and who worked mainly for the wealthy and famous in Beverly Hills, based at the Cedars Sinai Hospital. But when Dr. Reiss was not catering for their needs he spent a portion of his time serving the very poor of the community. As it happened, Bonnie had already come across this man through the assistance in midwifery that she had given Scientology members in the past. Dr. Reiss decided that Bonnie should be cared for under the program he undertook for the poor, and insisted that Bonnie be operated on the hospital in Beverly Hills where he was a consultant.

I sped across Los Angeles to the hospital as soon as I found out what was going on, my car filled with as many flowers as I could afford to buy, not knowing if the operation would be successful or not, shouting out loud in the car to anyone who I thought might be listening 'Don't let anything happen to her, she's my friend and I'm only just getting to know her. Don't take her now'.

After a successful operation Dr Reiss the surgeon came out of the operating theatre and told me that they had taken the equivalent of a basketball sized tumour out of Bonnie's abdomen, but she was okay and in recovery. I was so relieved that I wept. Bonnie stayed for about two weeks in hospital in recovery and then was allowed home to convalesce. But she didn't go back to the Scientology communal rooms she shared with her husband. She went instead to Geoffrey's apartment and convalesced there. Later she moved from Geoff's to accommodation offered to her from a Scientology member who she had helped in the past, a friendly guy called Martin, and there she sheltered from the Scientologists for about three months safely without the Organisation knowing. We saw each other every day and our love grew.

Then she had to move again. She was offered what we thought would be another safe location, even though we knew the people who owned it were former Scientologists. But for whatever reason they reported Bonnie's move to the Organisation, who in turn placed so much pressure on them that they told Bonnie she could no longer stay.

It was at this point I had managed to find an apartment and we started to share our lives together. After Bonnie's divorce came through we were free to marry. But although we didn't know it at the time, our marriage plans proved to be not as straightforward as we then thought.

After Bonnie left Bob, he quickly applied for and was granted a Mexican Divorce, which was something that other Scientologists had often done in the past. Although it seemed to be a reasonably common practise amongst Scientologists, Bonnie's lawyer thought it was a fairly dubious one, and open to contention as to its validity. So when Bonnie and I wanted to marry she filed for a Californian Divorce, not realising there was a six-month waiting period before we could legally marry. So when we did marry in March 1985 at Huntington Gardens, Pasadena we thought we were free to do so. Immediately after the wedding we spent some time in Ohio visiting Bonnie's family. We then moved to the East Coast for a while after before moving back to England in May 1985, where I started working in the building trade, on a self-employed basis.

But years later, when the private detectives hired by Scientology to investigate our past came across the Mexican and Californian divorce confusion that we had experienced, they reported us to the police at East Grinstead, Sussex, where we then lived, accusing us of bigamy! Our solicitor said it would be best to remarry. So our dear minister at that time, Charlie Crane at Trinity Methodist Church, remarried us.

Now I was back in England it was easier to be in regular touch with both my brother John and his family, and my mother, who had lived on her own since Dad's death. However I was more than a little surprised when one morning in 1992 I received an early morning call from my her. She didn't normally call at that time of the day, and if she needed anything it would be my brother who she would initially contact. She told me that she had been up all night, due to a chest infection, and was not feeling at all well.

Both Bonnie and I went round to see her, then called the doctor and waited for him to come and then made sure she had the medication the doctor prescribed before leaving again to get on with the day's business. Before leaving we promised that we would be back at four o'clock to get her some tea. But when we returned, she had already been taken to the hospital. Returning to the house, and finding it empty was a very strange experience – a bit like it might have been for those sailors who boarded the Marie Celeste who found the vessel just as though someone had abandoned it moments before their arrival. Everything of hers was there of course, just as though she had stepped out of the house for a few moments, including the telephone that was lying on the bed, where she had last used it. Then an hour later I received a call from John to say that she had died. She had apparently suffered a heart attack while talking to my sister-in-law Jean on the telephone and had died instantly.

That night, in spite of the traumatic events of the day, I fell into a deep sleep immediately after going to bed. Then I had a vision of both my mum and dad. They were together and they were smiling at me. They were both young and vibrant, and looked immensely happy stood against a back-drop of vivid green fields and blue sky. From that moment on I never doubted that the Lord had taken them both to be with Him.

This was not the first time that I had had an encounter with the things of God. Once in the early hours of the morning when I was just a little boy of about three or four I suddenly woke up. I knew the approximate time because the streetlights outside had gone out, as had the light on the landing, indicating that my parents had also retired for the night.

The reason for my sudden wakefulness was a very bright light which was lighting up the landing in its brilliance. I was fascinated. It was a far brighter light than the normal glow of the landing light. It was not at all like any light that I had seen before. Feeling quite unafraid, I crept out of bed, to see what was going on. As I got to the landing, the light appeared to travel down the stairs. I looked to see the source of this wonderful light. Then I saw Jesus, looking up at me! The light was all around Him, and He had His arms held wide in a beckoning gesture. I didn't speak – neither did He, and after a little while I went back to bed, not quite sure what to make of it all, but knowing that something signifi-cant had happened to me.

It was many years later, just about a year before my Mum died that something even more significant was to happen first to Bonnie and then to me, which would change us both forever. The change would bring both pleasure, pain and pressures such as we had never known before. But from that point on, we would never have to fight in our own strength again.

Chapter Six

Making The Break

I couldn't have known when I first met Richard, just how much my life was going to change in the next few years. Although at that point I was totally immersed in the teaching and philosophy of Scientology and all of my waking thoughts were dominated by their way of approaching life, I would soon find myself questioning everything that they stood for, and in doing so, reject it all. But in the process I would lose the last little bit of relationship that I had with Bob, and as humble as it was, a place to live, and even for a little while my daughter Desiree.

As Richard said in the last chapter, it was sickness that triggered these major changes in my life. I became so ill that circumstances took over, and my dear friend Geoff made the moves that undoubtedly saved me from dying.

After I left hospital I returned to Geoffrey's flat to recuperate. I had been told that recovery would take some time, and given that fact I didn't want to make any false moves. The operation that I had undergone had put in doubt any possibility of me giving birth to a child, and I so wanted to give my adopted daughter Desiree a brother or sister at some point in the future.

After the almost total restriction that I had lived under for the last few years, the total freedom I now enjoyed was over-whelming. Instead of being told what to do, what to think, what to wear and what to eat, it was again up to me to make these daily choices. I found myself missing the strong influ-ence the Scientologists had had on my life, and began to feel anxious that I had made the wrong decision in moving outside of their control, and wondered if I would face the consequences of my action for eternity. What I didn't know at that point was that guilt induction is part and parcel of a recovering cult member's thinking process.

But the overriding factor that would drive me back to communal living in our room in the Fountain building was my concern for Desiree. I hated the idea of not seeing her every day, and the dilemma of not being able to lift her or provide the care she needed as a lively four year old seemed unsolvable.

There seemed to be no way out, other than to return to Bob and my one room in the Fountain building. At least then I reasoned I would see her each morning before Bob took her to the nursery. When I put the idea to Geoff he was less than enthusiastic.

'Bonnie – are you crazy or what?' he said in exasperation. 'I can't believe what I'm hearing. You can't be serious! How on earth are you going to be looked after in those condi-tions?'

He had a point. And the conditions that I was planning to return to were only one side of the equation. I knew that I would face disciplinary action as soon as the Sea Org people thought I was physically able to do the amends proj-ects that would be required to make up for my 'unauthorised leave'. Yet I couldn't see any other way. In the back of my mind I told myself that it would only be a temporary measure, deciding that as soon as I was well enough I would let them know that I was leaving and taking Desiree with me. I knew that Bob would not be part of my future, as he had already told me that if I left I would do so without him.

Despite the fact that I had only minimum contact with my family during my time with Scientology I knew I only had to make one phone call and plane tickets would be on their way to me. But in spite of that knowledge, something held me back from phoning them. I decided instead that I needed to make Bob understand how unsuitable the place was for Desiree. When I broached the subject a few days later he made the astonishing remark that he had thought that I might not survive the operation and consequently hadn't given much thought to the marriage counselling or resolving our differences at all!

His remarks were like a spiritual slap in the face – and had the effect of bringing me to my senses, just like a phys- ical slap on the face sometimes calms down an hysterical person. I was suddenly able to see the bigger picture, and knew that there was absolutely no future staying there. As soon as that happened I couldn't do anything other than act on the knowledge I now possessed. I quickly dressed in the only pair of jeans and top I owned, put the spare change I found by the bedside table in my pocket, and told Bob that I was leaving, and that I would make arrangements to move Desiree out as soon as I was physically well enough to care and support her.

'And I want to make it quite clear that I trust you to see that Desiree remains safe, and I hold you completely accountable for that' I said to Bob in a voice a little less firm that I wanted it to be. I then walked quickly to the front door, and as I closed it behind me I heard it click, which reminded me that I had not taken a key with me, and therefore there would be no going back on the action I was now taking.

Now what should I do? I simply had no idea. Sitting on the front steps of the building, in the heart of Hollywood, I was at a loss to know what my next course of action should be. So I just sat there is a kind of daze, which as it turned out, was the best thing I could have done. Suddenly a car pulled up, and a man stuck his head out of the car window, and said, 'Hi Bonnie-can I give you a lift anywhere?'

I looked at him closer, and realised that it was Martin, a Scientologist for whom I had arranged some auditing during my time as Director of Processing. I remembered Martin as a talented musician, with a kind heart. Walking over to the car, and sticking my head through the open car window I suddenly found myself pouring out all my troubles to him, with him listening intently to what I had to tell him between my sobs. He thought for a moment and then with a warm smile on his face said, 'Well, this situation might just benefit us both.'

Seeing my quizzical look he continued, 'I've got to go to Florida in order to advance up a few levels, and I've been concerned about leaving my expensive musical instruments in the flat unattended. But if you were able to flat sit for me, that would solve your problem and mine.'

Without more ado, and with my jaw still scraping the ground in surprise at this sudden turn in events, he told me to get in the car.

'I have one or two things to arrange, which will take an hour or two. Once they are sorted I'll drive you to my flat. Meanwhile, have you had breakfast? I'm going to take you to a restaurant that I know where you can sit and eat while I get things organised.'

I couldn't quite believe that things were sorting themselves out so quickly, and yet I was relieved that they were. It seemed more like something out of one of the scripts written in Hollywood than actual life, but it was happening, so I just needed to let it happen, I told myself. Soon Martin was dropping me off at a local restaurant, where I used my last quarter to call Richard, who lived about an hour away, to tell him what had occurred.

'Order the biggest grand-slam breakfast they do,' he insisted, 'and tell the waitress I'll pay the bill when I arrive!'

By the time evening came I was safely ensconced in Martin's amazing little one bed roomed house in the middle of a residential park for the elderly. Not that Martin was elderly, but he liked the quiet environment which helped him compose and practise. Richard, Geoffrey and Martin then became my three Musketeers, thinking of everything I would need to have the proper six-week recovery time that had been ordered by the medics. To enable them to do the job properly though, they had had to use some delaying tactics. So as Richard and I were on the way to the house, he suddenly insisted that we stop off for a Baskin and Robbins ice cream knowing that the peanut butter and jelly flavour was an irresistible favourite of mine! Little did I know that he was actually stalling me so that the refrigerator could be well stocked with food!

The flat was everything I could have wished for – plus! I was thrilled every time the front door was opened in an evening by the wonderful perfume of flowering privet and heady gardenia which wafted in, in a most delightful way. My only sadness was that no children were allowed in the complex, so I made arrangements to take Desiree out every Saturday and Sunday until I was better, which Bob agreed to.

I began to enjoy some wonderful days of peace, safety and a growing confidence that I could survive everything that had happened and have a fresh start in life. But niggling in the background was the thought that ultimately the only way forward would be to make amends to the Scientologists for leaving their control, and in that way I would not be expelled from the group, and maybe stay in good standing with them, so that they would not declare me to be a Suppressive Person. I just couldn't take the risk of Bob having to disconnect when Desiree was living with him.

Then the peace that I was so enjoying was shattered one morning about six weeks later by a phone call that I was half expecting and half dreading. It was from the Scientology Ethics Officer, insisting that I go to see him immediately. How I wished that I had never picked up the phone. I didn't know what to say. I didn't even have Richard to advise me, as he was caught up with sales calls on the other side of town. Although I didn't want to attend this meeting, I thought that at least it would bring an end to the worry I had had about what would happen when they eventually found me. I agreed to see him at the Complex as soon as I could get down there.

When I arrived I was told to sit on a couch in the outer office until he was free. It seemed like hours before I was told I could go into his office. When I did I was promptly handed an Expulsion Order, the very thing that I had been dreading. He spelt out in no uncertain terms the way things would now proceed.

'A copy of this document will be sent to the International Justice Chief for his final approval' he said, studying my face for any reaction. Changing his tone slightly he continued 'Wouldn't it be easier just to return to the base and move back with your husband and child?. I can't see how you could possibly consider anything else'.

For once, words failed me. The thought of giving up all that I had gained in order to return to all that I had escaped from appalled me. I just grabbed the document and ran – and just managed to hear him say as I was sprinting out of his office 'if you want to change your mind you need to be quick – I'm going to send it off in the next post.'

I just needed to get out of that awful building, and speak to Richard as soon as possible. He'd know what to do, I had no doubt about that. I didn't stop running until I was half a block away, when I spotted a phone box which was empty. It was only when I got inside that I realised that I didn't have a cent on me, so phoning anyone was impossible! Now what could I do? My mind was racing so fast, that I couldn't think straight. All I knew was that I needed to speak to Richard, but there seemed no way that I was going to be able to do that until he returned home that evening.

I stood in the phone box, trying to collect my thoughts and half noticed a car pull up at the curb – then I realised it was Richard's car! He was looking at me as though I was a ghost. Then he jumped out of the car and ran towards me asking as he did, if I was OK.

'Richard' I stuttered 'how... what.. I mean – Richard, what are you doing here – how did you find me'.

'Bonnie – never mind about that now – just tell me what's going on.' I quickly explained to him my meeting with the Ethics Officer and his ultimatum to me, and without hesitation Richard said 'Jump in the car – I need to have a word with that ... er gentleman!'

After driving round to the Blue Building at some considerable speed, Richard jumped out of the car and stormed in the building with me following. When confronted by one of the receptionists who started to ask about the nature of his business I was startled to hear this very English man say firmly to them in true American fashion 'Shut up'! Up to that point Richard had always acted like a true English gentleman, almost like someone out of a fairy-tale. I was now seeing a different side to him – and I liked it! A lot! He stormed down the corridor with me in tow, and when he got to the office that I had left just minutes before he went straight in without waiting to be announced or summoned – no waiting on the couch for him!

He threw my copy of the now completely crumpled Ethics order on the big wide desk that was really the only furniture in the room and asked with feeling, 'Is this your rubbish?'

I was feeling pretty brave by this point, stood as I was behind Richard's broad and protective back, and so I peeked round him to interpret to the Ethics Officer that 'rubbish' was the English word for 'garbage'!

Neither man acknowledged my skills of interpretation, as Richard was continuing with his dialogue with the shocked official.

He told the man the terms he had to agree to concerning my departure, that my access to Desiree was to be whenever and however I wished, and that any non co-operation on his part might result in his lights being punched out! I figured that I need not interpret that one! Then, taking my hand, and without waiting for a reply, he walked out of the office, and out of the building without a backward glance. In those few moments my life stopped moving on the Scientologist's Bridge to Total Freedom, and started on the road which would ultimately bring me into real, lasting freedom.

As thrilled as I was about what had transpired, there was one thing that just didn't add up. How did Richard suddenly turn up, just at the point when I needed him the most? I was intrigued. The explanation that he gave me as we made our way back to my place was surely an indication that God had already started to intervene in both of our lives.

'I was driving on the Hollywood Freeway' he began, 'and all I was thinking about really was the number of sales calls I had to get through that day. Then, all of a sudden it seemed like someone else was driving the car – Bonnie, I've never experienced anything like it before. Before I knew it I was driving in the direction of the Scientology complex. I kept thinking you were in some kind of trouble, although my mind told me that you were back home at the apartment. I just started turning down various streets near to the Blue Building when I suddenly saw you in the phone box.'

There was no way that either of us could explain what had made Richard take that course of action – but it was one of many times that I saw God's hand at work in my life.

From that day forward I had access to Desiree whenever I wanted and a few months later, after separating from Bob and getting a job as an assistant manageress in a patisserie, I was able to take care of Desiree myself. She came to live with me and Richard and we enrolled her in a wonderful Montessori nursery school close to where I worked.

My life started to become wonderfully normal! I loved my job at the patisserie, and was taught how to bake all the items we sold. George, the owner of the shop was just great. Some days he used to pick up Desiree from school in his bright red sports car, which she loved, and on Saturday afternoon he would close the shop early to prepare a huge gourmet dinner for us.

But the best thing was not being told what to do my others – a common trait that cult organisations have towards their members. Unless you have been unfortunate enough to experience the restrictions that come with belonging to a cult, it is difficult to imagine the delight that comes from being free to go to bed three hours early if you want to, curling up on a sofa and reading a book, or just walking along the seafront with no particular place to go.

Although at this stage I was very much aware of the restrictions that Scientology had put upon me, I was still largely unaware of the dangers of Scientology. I had not yet fully grasped how ones whole lifestyle and worldview is determined by a set of rules and ways of thinking which are so strictly defined that no room is left for any choice or opinion at all.

Richard and I were keen to find a place of our own. That turned out to be an apartment in Hollywood very close to Griffith Park. A favourite treat was to drive up to the Observatory at dusk to watch all the lights come on over town, making the whole skyline look wonderfully different.

The park itself held even greater delights for Desiree and Ben, who we were able to have for the weekend sometimes as part of the access arrangement that Richard had with Elizabeth. We often went to the Park on a Saturday afternoon to ride the ponies or the train. But we always saved the best for last – climbing aboard the merry–go-round! The huge wooden Victorian horses were individually painted and it was always a difficult thing to know which one to choose to ride. That simple act will always stay in my mind as a symbol of my new found freedom. We always felt a bit sad each year as they closed down the shutters for the winter.

The Christmas of 1983 was very different from the one when we had first met. A lot had happened to change the way my mind was working – but I also began to realise that other things were changing about me too. Like my weight! I wasn't really eating any differently, yet I seemed to be piling on the pounds. Then, I woke up on Christmas Eve feeling very ill. 'Fine time to have flu,' I thought to myself, as I struggled not to throw up. As the day wore on I eventually began to feel better.

But it was when, just a couple of weeks later, that I had to buy a larger size pair of jeans for myself, that Richard decided it was high time I took a pregnancy test! I hated the idea of being disappointed by taking a test that might prove negative, as I had been trying to have children for so many years. But he thought of the best bribe he could to get me near the place where a test could be carried out – a visit to the English tearoom I loved in Santa Monica. After a lovely afternoon tea, on the way home we 'just happened' to pass a Planned Parenthood centre!

As we sat in the reception area, surrounded by several distressed teenage girls, I was more than a little nervous. When we were called in to see the advisor she was astonished to find that we had waited this long to come in – I was by this time about six weeks pregnant and was informed that the baby would arrive in September! To say at that point that I was ecstatic would be an understatement.

Dr. Reiss, who had performed the operation when Geoffrey had taken me to the hospital, was away in Israel, but Richard tracked him down and told him the news. The doctor advised me to be extra careful due to the surgical measures he had taken, and added that he wanted to see me in two weeks time. From then on he saw me every fortnight until the baby was born.

Once our friends learned of our news some kept asking us when we were going to get married. I stubbornly refused to even consider the idea of a 'shotgun wedding'. Richard still likes to call me Annie Oakley when I get in this kind of frame of mind!

Andreanna Edith Ruby Woods was born on the first of September, when is traditionally known as Labour Day in the United States. Well, for us it was Labour Day in a personal as well as a national sense! The other memorable thing about that day was that it turned out to be one of the hottest days of the year -105 degrees in the shade!

Richard had taken a series of special classes so that he could be in the operating room, in case I needed a Caesarean Section. Andreanna made her first appearance around 5 am and from that moment on there was hardly an hour that Richard wasn't holding her. He became a familiar sight in those corridors wheeling her bassinet to the nursery, as the babies had to return there each day during visiting hours. The nurses even pulled a rocking chair close to her cot for him.

I'm sure that her birth brought him great joy but it must have been tinged with the bittersweet memories of his time in hospital with his baby daughter Rebecca born to his first wife who had died so young because of a heart problem. We didn't understand it then but God was already starting to restore the joy and life that had been stolen from us.

After a few days we brought Andreanna home to our apartment and although there wasn't a lot of space for the four of us, we were very happy there. Richard had been offered a job supervising the installation of kitchens and he really enjoyed trouble shooting the work. He really respected the contractor he worked with and they in turn were able to find a cabinet company that produced beautiful solid wood components. For a while, life seemed to be moving along smoothly. Then the contractor ran into some serious cash flow problems and he had to wind down the company very abruptly.

I was pleased and surprised to see Richard return home early on a beautiful spring afternoon. He quickly told me the state of the company. But what he then said made me think even harder.

'This probably sounds crazy to you Bonnie, but, well, in spite of everything that we have here, the lovely climate, the freedom, you know, everything that America stands for, I'm sort of missing England.' He looked at me hard, to try to gauge my reaction, but I was too intent on taking in what he was saying to register anything.

'And I was just kind of wondering if, well, what you might think about moving there?' He might have thought I would be shocked, but in fact I thought it to be a pretty exciting idea. I'd studied English Literature at college which had given me a love for England.

'Sounds like a great idea to me' I said with a grin, watching his features change from concern to a look of delight. So it was settled – we were bound for good old England! And if that was the case I decided, there was no time like the present to start making arrangements. The very next weekend saw the first of several garage sales, when the things that we couldn't take with us to England were sold at a knockdown price to our friends and neighbours. In my enthusiasm to clear everything that we weren't able to take with us, I managed to sell our bed two weeks before we were due to leave the country!

Now the inquiries about our wedding plans seemed to be more relevant than they had been when our baby was born. There were more reasons for us to be married than not, so a wedding was the next obvious step. We decided that the venue should be one of our favourite places – the Shakespeare garden at the Huntington Botanical Gardens in Pasadena. But we knew that we also needed someone to perform the ceremony. I looked in the telephone directory and found a lady minister by the name of Eunice, who, when I contacted her was able and free on the day we had chosen.

Neither Richard nor I knew much about the Christian church in those days, and the fact that Sister Eunice was of the Pentecostal persuasion meant little to us. We were therefore a little taken aback by the fervent way she prayed for us both during the service, but looking back now I can see how very blessed we were to have that kind of start to our married life together.

Somehow we managed to pack everything we wanted to take with us in five huge suitcases and we flew to Ohio to spend a few weeks with my family before completing our journey to England. Mom was thrilled to meet Richard, and from that day forward she always referred to him as Lionheart! I was worried that she would be upset that we were moving so far away but she gave us some very wise advice that has been one of the principles we have built our marriage on. She quoted the book of Ruth and told me that 'whithersover he goes, so will you'. And I have always believed that my home is where he is.

We settled on the south coast of England in a little village called East Preston and I was fascinated by the seafront. Richard grew up in Worthing so he was quite matter of fact about things which I found astonishing. The very first evening we went for a walk and I spotted a red phone box. He couldn't pry me out of it for some time. We took long walks on footpaths that climbed the Downs and sheltered with a whole herd of cows, under a massive oak tree during a rainstorm. We had lunch in country pubs with roaring fires and ale from the cask that left us a bit confused about which path to take back to the car!

It rained solidly for the first twenty-five days I spent in this country so Richard immediately took me shopping for a grey raincoat with matching umbrella and hat. I wasn't so sure if I'd made the right decision in moving to the land of my husband's birth as I looked out of the long windows of our flat at another grey day. But the first glorious days of May made me forget all that. Before I came to Britain I thought the idea of a lark's song was something someone imagined until I saw and heard one for myself as we squelched through marshlands that first spring.

We now seemed so far removed in time and space from Los Angeles and I would have been content to wipe those times from my memory altogether. But God had other plans and another purpose in mind for me.

Chapter Seven

Angels Watching Over Me

For me, living in the little village of East Preston after Los Angeles was like stepping back in time! If I didn't focus on the car registration numbers I could have easily convinced myself that I had somehow gone back to the year 1946! The pace and attitude to life was just how it used to be many years before in the USA. I felt I was in my own cosy little time warp – until I went shopping!

We lived for a time in a flat above the shops in the High Street, and I discovered that I was known as the token Yank! I wondered why the shopkeepers, as they got to know me better, seemed to become more offensive in the way they spoke to me.

'I see you were busy bombing Saddam again last night' the hardware store owner said as I walked through the door one morning. 'Excuse me?' I said, realising that he could only be talking to me, as I was his one and only customer. He grinned and asked me what I wanted to buy. What was he talking about, I wondered with more than a little irritation? I knew the American Air force were involved in a bombing campaign against Iraq, but this guy was making out that I was personally responsible!

'Why is he being so nasty to me' I wailed to Richard

when he got home that night. 'He surely can't believe that all that horrible bombing has got anything to do with me'?

Richard put down his newspaper and carefully explained the English trait of using sarcasm as a form of endearment. 'He's saying those kind of things, because he wants to be friendly,' said Richard with a grin. 'What you need to do is to think of something equally outrageous to say back to him.' I opened my mouth to object but Richard had already anticipated my response. 'Yes, I know in America that would be terribly rude, but that's the way it works over here, believe me.'

Well, they say when in Rome...... but I knew I needed to psyche myself up for this one. The next morning I went in to the shop again but this time I was prepared for a verbal battle. 'Bombing went well last night did it Mrs. Woods?, the hardware store owner asked as I stepped through the door. I was ready for him.

'Actually, I have to say that I've never been involved in the bombing of Iraq – or anywhere else for that matter. But if I were to start, this island would be my prime target – it might improve the weather!' Then I quickly added, 'Do you have a clothes drier I could buy from you'?

'Of course, Mrs. Woods,' he said, his eyes sparkling. When I had paid for this piece of equipment that I hoped would dry some of our clothes in the impossibly wet British climate that I was battling with, he even escorted me to the shop door, carrying the large awkward box for me! In spite of my rudeness and verbal onslaught he couldn't have been nicer! In a trice I had turned in his eyes from an American wimp, keen to please and be polite, to one of the locals, ready to give as good as I got. So this was how the game was played! I was getting to know the English. I wondered what my friends back home would have made of the conversation

I had just had. I was getting to know the people of my new country of adoption. But their food was something else.

Thanksgiving Day was just around the corner, and I wanted to make a favourite family dish called Sunshine Salad, an old family recipe that we had with Thanksgiving and Christmas dinner in my mother's family. It's a savoury/sweet salad made with jello, or as the British insist on calling it jam. The other ingredients were grated carrots, celery, mandarin oranges, pineapple, apple and sometimes walnuts. I get nostalgic for home every time I taste it, although I have to admit that Richard could take it or leave it – and mainly he would choose to leave it!

I couldn't find any jello, only something called jelly which I guessed was the same, but with a slightly different spelling. Pleased with my find, I bought 12 packs. When I opened them up I was mystified why this English jello came in funny little cubes which tasted much too strong, and was very chewy! But I dutifully lined a large roasting tin with them vainly trying to smooth them out, until Richard came home from work and saw what I was up to and explained my mistake. I had a lot to learn!

Our house was just a ten-minute walk from the sea and I spent hours with Desiree and Andreanna exploring the part of the beach nearest to where we were living. Those times with the girls marked the beginning of a healing process that had been divinely designed.

I had never spoken the word 'Scientology' to anyone out loud since coming to live in England – quite a feat really as the Scientologist's terminology for describing all aspects of life became second nature after being with them for a while. But although my words were no longer dominated by Scientology jargon it was a different matter as far as my thought processes were concerned. I interpreted the behaviour of everyone I met according to Scientology theories and principles. So if I heard someone criticising anyone else I always presumed it was because they had in some way betrayed that person, perhaps without them even knowing about it, and as a result were now only able to speak critically about them. Old thought patterns take time to break. Scientology teaching says that if a person becomes critical of another person or activity it can be traced to undisclosed transgressions against that person or thing. These are called withholds. It is always presumed in Scientology that any critical remark about another stems from the existence of harmful acts that have been previously committed against the other person of which quite possibly they are unaware. These harmful acts are called overts. If you accumulate too many overts and withholds against another person it might eventually cause you to refuse communication with them altogether. Much of the time spent in Scientology processing or auditing concentrates on searching for and discovering these transgressions committed in this or earlier lifetimes.

The Scientology mindset reminded me of a childhood game I received one Christmas in my stocking. It was called 'Pick-up Sticks'. You had a good-sized cylinder of multi-coloured plastic sticks which you tossed in a heap on the table. The object of the game was to carefully withdraw the sticks without collapsing the heap. The spring of 1990 saw the bundle of sticks that comprised my emotional life collapse and scatter in several directions.

I had never really comprehended how far away from home I was and I had only been home twice in all that time. Then my mother contracted pneumonia and my sister called me late one afternoon desperate for me to come back right away. I flew to Boston that evening but as I raced across the terminal to catch a connecting flight, I somehow knew in my heart that I would be too late to see her before she died.

In the early hours of the next morning, after spending a fair amount of time with my grieving family I stretched out on Mom's bed and tried to sleep. I thought at the time I was dreaming, but on reflection I believe that I saw a vision. Mom was standing in the most brilliant green field I have ever seen in what I guess must have been early springtime. The other colours that I could see – red, yellow and blue were of an intensity I've never seen before or since. Mom was young again, probably in her thirties. I knew that because I had often seen pictures of her at that age around the time I was born. I also knew with certainty as I looked at her that she was in a place of safety, but I was filled with such a great sadness because it was a place that I didn't know how to get to myself.

I returned to England in a state of shock that lasted about six months. I didn't come to terms with Mom's death at all and I would often purchase some souvenir for her when we visited somewhere new to me. Before she died we used to speak to each other every Sunday afternoon at 4 o'clock and even though she was now dead I still insisted we couldn't leave the house during that time. Richard tried to gently remind me that she was gone but I wouldn't have any of it.

Then Andreanna's birthday came around, and when of course she didn't receive a birthday card from Mom, the house of cards I'd built in my mind fell down. I spent the next month in the darkness of depression.

I was inconsolable and seemed to be crying constantly. My only respite was reading – I think I must have got 50 or 60 books out of the library during the next four week period. I didn't eat or sleep very much but each day Richard would pack peanut butter and jam sandwiches for me and I would walk for miles and miles on the seafront. I attended many early morning wake-up calls with the sea gulls often seeing them perform feats that would be brilliant material for a really amazing nature film.

Richard showed his great love for me and the girls during this terrible time. To add to my other problems I also became very agoraphobic, so he was left with taking the girls to and from school and preparing all the meals and coping with laundry and everything else. How he managed to continue running his building business as well I'm not quite sure. I used to plead with him to send me to hospital where I felt maybe they would have a cure, but he was very wise in declining to do so, as he felt sure that he would never find a doctor who would understand what I had been through. His love for me and the girls and his determination to keep me safe is the foundation of our relationship and I know that unconditional love it is the key to helping others recover.

I had two good and faithful friends at the time. Ann, who was originally from London, was the first friend I made in Worthing. She was someone who had an extraordinary ability to listen and understand and although I had no idea at the time, she prayed for me for years. My other friend was called Janet. We met at a cookery class I started to attend, and Janet went out of her way for years to be steadfast in her affection and concern for me. During my lowest point she was the only person I would open the front door to. We would sit and have a coffee together and somehow, impossibly, she would be able to make me laugh.

Then one afternoon, on the 28th of September 1990, to be precise, I was sitting on the stairs at home and I started to scream at God, actually speaking directly to Him for the first time since I had been a young child. Giving vent to some of the pain and misery that had been building up in me I shouted, 'What have you done with my mother?'

Now if you are not familiar with guardian angels you might find this next bit hard going but its what happened to me and it made the difference between night and day in my world then. I had no sooner got the words out of my mouth when I had someone sit down next to me and reassuringly put an arm around my shoulders, and say 'She's absolutely fine, she's just asleep.' I knew that person immediately, as well as I know any of my closest friends. Every night of my early childhood my mother had prayed with me that I would be guarded by my angels while I slept. She would describe them and did it so well that had I the artistic skill I could show you how I imagined the angels would look. The one who came to sit with me on the stairs was just like the one Mom had described – it was one and the same. As you can imagine I was pretty freaked out and by the time Richard came home from work, I thought perhaps I was becoming delusional. But then strange delusions don't heal a person's mind. This was different.

The next morning when I woke up I felt perfectly fine and I jumped out of bed, made breakfast, dressed the girls for school and ordered some tickets to a Big Band concert for the next evening to celebrate Richard's birthday which was that day! I was beginning to discover how much God loves us first and how Jesus, the Good Shepherd seeks the lost.

Then Janet popped round one afternoon, and asked if I would like to go to a dinner to be held in one of the local hotels. 'After the meal, they'll have a speaker, who'll be talking about how God has influenced his life,' said Janet smiling. 'It would be great if you could come along.'

I thanked Janet, and said it sounded interesting, surprised

to find that she had 'religious' connections. It turned out that Barry her husband was President of the organisation that was hosting the dinner, something called The Full Gospel Businessmen's Fellowship International. I went along, partly because of my friendship with Janet, and partly out of curiosity. We all sat at tables which seated about eight people, and were served a nice chicken dinner and a light sweet, before the guest speaker rose to his feet.

He gave a moving and interesting talk, before inviting people to come to the front for prayer. I noticed that some of them were in tears, and Janet was by their side, speaking a word of comfort to them. Before I left, Janet's husband Barry gave me a book called The Happiest People on Earth written by the man who founded the Full Gospel Businessmen's Movement, Demos Shakarian.

'So why was everyone in tears, if they're supposed to be the happiest people on earth?' asked Richard who was obviously puzzled after I had tried to explain to him what the evening was like when I got home.

'Well, I don't know why they were so tearful, but maybe this book will explain. Anyway, it sounds as though the people in the book are happy, but that could be because they're living in California,' I reasoned.

Getting interested in the book was no problem at all. It had a light and easy style, and I enjoyed reading about the author's encounters with God. But alongside that book I found myself reading the Gospel of John. In fact, I couldn't get enough of it. What I started to read was fascinating as I had never really read the Bible in context before, but I found the stories about Jesus perplexing as His miracles were described in such a matter of fact fashion. I wanted to read John's Gospel more than the five or six other books I had on the go at any one time.

Janet started to help us in the office with the bookkeeping associated with Richard's building work, and a spin off from that was that we began to get to know her husband Barry better too. One morning he asked Richard if he could drop by to tell him about a business plan that would be of great benefit to him. 'It's probably about insurance,' said Richard as he told me about the meeting that had been arranged later that morning. We both had an idea that that was Barry's line of business.

At the given hour Barry arrived, and sat patiently waiting for Richard to end his interminable phone calls. But when Richard finally appeared outside his office to join Barry and me in the reception area, instead of giving us some insurance spiel, Barry started to describe how very interested God was in our lives. He told us what had happened to Adam and Eve in the Garden of Eden, how they had been tempted, and how they had been betrayed and deceived.

I was fascinated by what he was saying – and intrigued by what I was physically experiencing as he spoke! It was as though someone had lit the ends of my feet with a blowtorch! I couldn't understand why I was feeling this way, and what it had to do with what Barry was saying. But as he spoke I began to understand for the first time the focus of all the teaching I had received in the convent schools I had attended. As Barry continued he gave the most impassioned description of how Jesus had been sacrificed for the whole world, and that God, through the death of Jesus, was offering a way out of all the pain and sorrow that is the result of Adam and Eve's sin. He said that all we had to do was to turn our business and our lives over to God, and He would take over the job of Senior Manager and would begin to resolve our problems.

I realised that Barry was speaking of the same Jesus that

I had been reading about each day in my Bible, as if He was standing in the room that very moment. It became clear all of a sudden to me that Jesus, the one I was fascinated by in the gospel stories, was still alive and was wanting to know about me!

The rest of the afternoon passed in a bit of a blur. I took a bus home to meet the girls after school, and the hour-long journey seemed to pass in five minutes.

Once home I sat down in the conservatory of my dream home by the sea and spoke to God about this plan of His to rescue our lives. In spite of the fact that Richard was working flat out we were on the edge of bankruptcy. And to complicate matters we currently owned two houses as we mistakenly thought we would have no difficulty selling one of them One had tenants in it, which we could do nothing about at that time,so we had reluctantly decided to sell my dream house. We would have preferred of course not to sell the home we had grown to love so much but finances dictated that we had no other option. I began to wonder just what the outcome would be.

Then I thought again about what Barry had said earlier that day. He seemed emphatic about the fact that if we turned everything over to God and trusted Him with our lives, He would be in charge from that point on, which meant we could stop worrying. I told God that in my opinion He was getting the raw side of the deal. However, if He really wanted my life He could have it! Then I prayed that He would take care of Richard and the girls, as I was putting their lives into His hands too. I knew that I was not able to protect them from the distress that we were all suffering at that time in different ways.

So that was that. It never occurred to me to tell anyone about the agreement that God and I had come to that

Wednesday afternoon or that it would be of interest to anyone other than me. God is so faithful and the same afternoon I listed the house with a local estate agent. Only a couple of hours later I had a call from the agent to say they had someone very interested in seeing the house. They came Saturday morning, and by late afternoon had made an offer we found acceptable under the circumstances. That result certainly grabbed my attention and it strengthened my idea that I could ask God to deal with other problems that came up. Now we needed to know where we were going to live.

I seemed to waste lots of time searching for a house to rent close to the business offices, armed with a list of amenities that Richard felt our new place ought to have. Although I contacted a whole list of Estate Agents I had absolutely no success. So I decided to ask Jesus, my Senior Partner, to deal with it and that same afternoon after calling an agent Janet had suggested, the agent told me about a house that sounded just right. When we went round to check it out, and the owner opened the front door, Richard found myself staring at his first cousin who he had last seen twenty years before! Needless to say, the house was just what we needed, and a deal was quickly struck. God certainly knows how to spring a surprise!

A couple of weeks later, I was invited to go along to another meeting that Barry and Janet had organised in a hall in the centre of town. They had told me that over the month's speakers from abroad as well as Britain came to talk about their faith and trust in God. I went along eagerly, interested in what they had to say.

The speaker that evening was Bob Barker, and as he spoke I was impressed with his Bible knowledge, as he quoted from books in the Bible that I had never even heard of! At the end of his talk he invited those who were suffering from depression to come to the front for prayer. Janet leaned over, and said that she would go out with me, if I wanted to be prayed for.

'Thanks Janet, but I'm fine' I whispered grateful for her kindness and friendship. But it was only as we were walking back to the car that I realised that for the first time in many, many months I was at peace and not troubled about anything.

Although I now had a peace which I could only have dreamed of a few weeks before, I knew that Richard was still worried about business things, which tended to make him feel depressed. So the morning after the meeting, I rang Janet, with whom I knew Bob Barker was staying overnight, and she invited me over for a coffee and a chat with Bob.

Bob was nothing if not forthright. His first words to me were 'Are you saved?'

'Saved from what?' I replied innocently. Seeing that I didn't understand what he was talking about he explained in simple terms the gospel message, how because of Adam's disobedience sin had entered the world, which had caused a separation between God and man. He went on to explain how Jesus' death on the cross dealt with the sin and there-fore the separation, and once we acknowledged what Jesus had done for us on the Cross, we could have an unhindered relationship with God, just as it was at the beginning of time.

He also told me how angry Satan feels towards people who turn to Jesus for salvation, messing up his diabolical plan of taking the human race with him to hell.

'But I've made my peace with God' I said, 'and it's been wonderful ever since'. Barry and Janet, who kept popping in and out of the kitchen as Bob and I spoke, seemed more than a little surprised by my disclosure. They were obviously delighted that their many prayers for me had born fruit, and I'll always be so grateful for their faithfulness, love and concern and for their determination to rescue me from the absolute spiritual darkness I was in.

Bob then offered to take me back home, so that he could have a word with Richard. As soon as we got there, the two men got into a discussion while I started to chat with Andreanna my seven year old daughter. I told her that Daddy was chatting to a man who loved Jesus, just like I now did.

'Mummy,' she said in a voice that I recognised would have a request coming into the sentence somewhere, 'can I have a Bible like yours, because I know Jesus, and want to read the stories about him!' I looked at her in astonishment. This was all news to me. I wanted to know more.

'Mummy, I been waiting so long for you to know Jesus – ever since my friends Ester and Rebecca told me about Him'.

What she was saying was news to me, but the names I recognised. Ester and Rebecca were two little girls who lived across the road from us when Andreanna was 4 years old. Ruth, their mother was Jewish, and the family had shown us great kindness during the time we lived near them, and Andreanna had often played with the girls. They attended a Church of England primary school, and shared with her the stories of Jesus that they had been told by their teachers!

'It would be great if Daddy got to know Jesus too, wouldn't it Mum? And I think it might happen – he doesn't mind reading Bible stories to me, does he?'

She was right. Each morning Andreanna would jump into bed with us, carrying her new picture Bible, and insist that Richard read the accompanying scripture from the story she chose. It seemed that this was her way of getting her Daddy interested in her special friend, Jesus!

My approach was not so subtle. Something marvellous had happened to me, and I wanted with all my heart for Richard to share in what I was enjoying. If I had had my way, I would have harangued him morning noon and night until he gave in, but that's not God's way and I eventually learned to lean on God for all that I need as well as the others, and to let Him direct the Save Richard operation!

But that's his story to tell.

The next few months found me immersed in the Bible, often spending four or five hours a day, or two or three hours in the early morning, praying and asking God to help me understand His will for my life. During one such prayer conversation with God, I asked Him how Scientology could be stopped, thinking about the damage that it had done in my life, and the lives of others that I knew.

As I prayed, I had a very clear impression that God wanted me to alert people to the dangers of Scientology which would of course involve stopping its progress. Needless to say I was none too pleased at the suggestion I seemed to be getting that I should try to rescue others from that maze of deception and darkness from which I had only so recently been delivered myself. But I wanted so very much to honour the agreement that God and I had made, and my life was now His. But what His plans would lead me into I could only guess.

Chapter Eight

The Truth Will See You Free

We need to step back now for a moment, to the time when I first began to see the truth about Scientology. As much as I enjoyed Britain, and was getting accustomed to its customs and its people, there was no way I wanted to turn my back on my own country and culture. 'After all,' I said to my friend Ann when we were having coffee together one morning, 'I don't want to deny my heritage, or where I've come from. It's very important to me.'

'Well, Bonnie, I know that,' she said in her strong London accent as she bit into a chocolate biscuit – 'and you're right too! Be true to yourself I always say.' Then after a slight pause she said 'But you know Bonnie, there are things about the UK you might like to give a go – like Radio 4 for instance!'

Now it was my turn to fall silent for a moment. Radio was not something I had given much thought to, apart from having it playing in the background as I drove around in the car. But Ann went on to explain how that particular radio station was mainly speech based, and might prove to be interesting to listen to as I did my housework. Little did she know how right her words would turn out to be!

The next morning found me lugging a music system

down from our bedroom and into the kitchen, where I was soon engaged in searching for the radio station she had mentioned. After a few minutes I picked up the clipped British accent of a BBC interviewer, half way through a discussion with a man called Russell Miller. As they chatted, it became clear that their talk was about a book Miller had written called The Bare Faced Messiah. The title meant nothing to me, but I decided to stay with the discussion anyway, as I proceeded to bake some cookies for Richard and the girls. Then, as I was blending the mixture together, I suddenly realised that the subject of the book was none other than L. Ron Hubbard! The interview ended by saying that the book was now available at all good bookshops!

My feet hardly touched the ground as I scooped up Andreanna from the floor where she had been contentedly playing with her toys, grabbed my purse and keys and ran down the street in order to catch the first available bus to the town centre of Worthing where I knew W. H. Smith's had a large book section.

Arriving at the counter in a somewhat breathless condition, I asked the assistant if they had Miller's book in stock. 'No, M'am' he said politely, then added 'but you could place an order, and we'd give you a ring when it comes in – it will probably take about two weeks.' The deal was done, but it was nearer three weeks before I managed to get into town and take it home with me.

Although I had been involved in Scientology for so long, this was the first time ever I had a book in my possession which actually told me the truth about the organisation. I was eager to know what had happened to my heart, soul and mind during the time I had been involved with them. But as I started to read what it had to say I was shocked with its disclosures and couldn't cope with the idea that the founder of Scientology could be talked about in such derogatory terms. Worse still, the book also contained Scientology teaching that the Scientologists had always said should be secret from anyone who had not reached a certain level on 'the Bridge'. I had been taught that exposure to those ideas could be physically and mentally dangerous to anyone who read them who hadn't been prepared to do so. I knew that I had reached a much higher level than Richard – what if he picked it up and started to read it, I wondered in panic. I decided the only thing I could do would be to hide the book away in a box of odds and ends in the airing cupboard, where Richard would never be likely to find it. There was no way I wanted him becoming mentally disturbed or contacting pneumonia as a result of reading it.

My concerns, although they probably sound far fetched, were based on real fears. When I had been deeply involved in Scientology I had sometimes supervised members who had suffered psychotic episodes, as a result, I was told, of their reading of OTIII materials. I had no reason to doubt what I was told at the time, and there was no way I was going to expose Richard to that kind of risk.

I should have been more prepared for the reaction that I had towards reading critical statements about the Scientology movement. I now know that people who have been subjected to the counselling and training methods of Scientology end up with an inbuilt protective mechanism which shuts down critical thinking when impartial evaluation of the subject is demanded. It's as though a fail-safe mechanism is implanted in the mind of a member to protect them from such information, or like doors which have been placed in their mind which start sealing off, with alarm bells ringing, making it far too uncomfortable for them to carry on with the examination of any material which is derogatory towards Scientology or its founder, Ron Hubbard, who is also known as Source. The whole process reminded me of one of those sequences in a science-fiction movie when something foreign penetrates a space capsule and all the warning systems start a countdown to destruct! But whatever the analogy, the end result is that Scientologists are programmed not to hear any criticism about the system or its founder, meaning that they can never truly revaluate what they have committed themselves to.

In the end I never actually read the book right through, partly because it was lost in a house move we had some time later. But one name which was mentioned in the book kept popping up in my mind. Russell Miller had credited someone called Jon Atack as the person responsible for some of the most damming evidence against Ron Hubbard, and I kept wondering 'What if I met him, and I could satisfy myself that the evidence he gave in the book was genuine'. The unanswered question kept raising to the surface every so often and I even went to the library on a couple of occasions and looked at telephone directories for East Grinstead, where the Scientologists had their international headquarters, scanning through them for the name of Jon Atack, but could never find any listing. I finally decided to put the whole idea at the back of my mind and not bother myself about it any more.

Soon I was distracted by another house move. Events were due to take a strange twist, after I wrote a letter to my old friend Geoffrey who was living still in L.A., giving him our East Preston address. He wrote back telling me of some friends he had who were living near to us, and suggested that I look them up.

So, a few days later I went to see the wife of Geoffrey's

friend who had invited me for coffee, and during the course of the conversation the subject of Scientology came up. I told her about the book I had bought, and was still wondering whether or not what Russell Miller had written could be true. Her reply had me staring at her in disbelief.

'You should ask Jon Atack about that – I have a friend who knows him and I'm sure she would give you his number!'

In spite of the fact that in the end I had stumbled upon Jon's number quite by chance, it would be another year before I phoned him up. There was a part of my mind that had what seemed like huge oak doors that would not unlock unless someone produced the right key. I didn't know it then, but I needed the protection of God's Holy Spirit before I ventured further into the reality of what lay behind Scientology, lest I was caught in a quicksand of spiritual danger.

So God made sure that by the time I first met Jon, who would be the means of me delving deeper into the roots of Scientology, I had already become a born-again believer in Jesus. And when I told some dear Christian friends of mine, Hazel and Jim about the plans I had to meet Jon for the first time, and what I hoped to achieve, Hazel offered to accompany me to Jon's house, an offer which I greatly appreciated. She met me at East Grinstead railway station, and as it was a fine day we decided to walk to Jon's house, looking forward to catching up on each other's news as we went.

But as we walked over the footbridge, we were suddenly aware of a cloud of bees or hornets that began to move around our heads, causing Hazel to hastily put up her umbrella. It was all rather odd. And something else, even odder had happened during my journey. As I was changing trains at Haywards Heath, I suddenly fell flat on my face, in the tunnel between platforms. Just clumsy? Maybe. But later I discovered that two people from my Fellowship felt it right to hold a prayer vigil in their car which was parked outside Jon's house for the whole time we were together. I also discovered that another group from the Fellowship, who were doing a prayer walk of the town had been led to pray outside his house, not even knowing he lived there, until Hazel pointed it out.

Jon and I don't share the same views on Christianity, but I found in him a friend who could understand the torment I had suffered, and who could offer comfort and answers to the many questions that I had carried around for years. Before leaving he gave me a copy of his book A Piece of Blue Sky, but as well as that I also took with me a reassurance that I could come again as often as I liked to inspect the research he had done, to verify for myself the truth of what he had written.

The next few months offered me a chance to review what seemed like thousands thousands of pages of documentation about Hubbard's early years and an agenda which he had, for the members of Scientology which I had been unaware of throughout my eight year involvement,. It had been easy to disregard what I had read in Bare-faced Messiah because Russell Miller was a journalist and I had been indoctrinated to believe that information from a source like that was not to be trusted. It was another matter altogether to be faced with Hubbard's own writings – randomly chosen from Jon's astonishing collection. I say randomly chosen because Jon made a point of not directing me to anything himself but only supplying documentation when I asked specific questions regarding aspects of the technology. I also had the freedom to delve into any of the documentation that he had – literally thousands of pages of material. Some of the Hubbard writings were contained in books which I was familiar with but had never looked at in the clear light of critical thinking. I was later to discover that an important aspect of exit counselling is of an information-providing nature, and its value lies in encouraging the member to draw independent conclusions, and not to interpret the material for them or try to persuade them to agree with your own opinions.

I offered to help Jon in any way I could. I now know that the help I was willing to give him was a rare occurrence as far as he was concerned. But having fully realised how much damage I had done to the people I had recruited into Scientology I was grateful for the opportunity to redress the situation by beginning to tell my experience to others whose lives hung in the balance. And so I offered to accompany Jon as he helped families who were hoping to present this kind of information to their loved ones and enable them to make a fully informed decision. I saw Jon spend countless hours patiently answering every query with a document, being reluctant to give a member his own opinion on the subject.

I was always struck by his compassion for their distress when they realised they had been misinformed and lied to by a group they had trusted. Then when I saw the lies Scientology published about Jon and the lengths they were prepared to go to destroy his credibility, I began to understand how costly my decision to speak the truth as I understood it would be.

Jon was the subject of several Scientology publications which contained similar allegations to the ones that would be made about me. They said that he was involved in 'deprogramming' which they defined in one of their Freedom magazines as

'a euphemism for a socially and morally immoral practice which involves a sustained mental and sometimes physical assault against a person's chosen religion. ...Often kidnapping and other forms of illegal restraint are used'.

He was named as part of a clique who were trying to upset and harass and use subterfuge to try and persuade Scientologists to leave their religion.

Shortly after my first meeting with Jon I was invited to speak to a group of ministers from East Grinstead and the surrounding communities who wanted to hear of my experiences with the Scientology movement and to share any information I had with them. It was the beginning of friendships, support and encouragement upon which to this day Richard and I depend. Soon I started to receive frequent requests from the media to describe my life as a Scientologist and I was naïve enough to think that surely the experiences of a middle-aged housewife would be of little interest to a worldwide organisation! Certainly if I was mistaken about what their founder had said they would be in the most ideal position to refute it. Once my name was on file with various media agencies it was easy for others in the profession to locate me. The idea that the media were seeking me out must have been a bitter pill for Scientology to swallow as throughout the litigation years they would be adamant that I had solicited press interest in my story.

By this time I was receiving an ever increasing numbers of phone calls from people worried about their family members and friends, because of their involvement with Scientology. I had shared my testimony with a Christian group called the Deo Gloria Trust who had quite a backlog of Christian families anxious for more information from another Christian who had personal experience with Scientology. The workload was increasing and I was longing for someone with whom to share the burdens.

Richard was still manning his building business and was very supportive and endeavoured to give me every opportunity to help as many people as I could. Meanwhile, God had been doing some building work of His own in Richard's life! Following my understanding with the Almighty, or to be more precise, my acknowledgement of Jesus as my Lord and Saviour, I had gone through the waters of baptism and Richard started to see a great deal of change taking place in me. I had been keen to have our wedding vows blessed – and Barry had agreed to a short, informal ceremony at the Ardington Hotel following the Sunday Service that our Fellowship held.

As we stood to receive the blessing, Janet brought a word from the Lord that she had received for Richard. It spoke of God's longing for Richard to hear His calling for him and how God had longed for him to seek His face.

Richard was overcome with God's love and it was fortunate that I'd been given a special handkerchief to mark the occasion because he certainly needed it! That incident was the start of us becoming fully committed to God's will as a family and I was blessed to witness my husband being truly smitten with a newfound love of Jesus. There is no greater joy than seeing your beloved assured of his place as a child of God.

Although we all now got a newfound faith in Jesus, it didn't mean that life was plain sailing. Often, when people give their lives to the Lord, and allow Him to take control of every aspect, there is a certain amount of sorting out to be done, which can sometimes be painful. This certainly was the way it was for us. Our house purchases and deals were a case in point. Looking back, it was all a bit like a giant monopoly game – and one we could have well done without playing!

The first house we purchased was in Worthing in 1987. We bought it in two stages, as at the time it was divided into an upstairs and downstairs flat. But Richard was able to convert it into a nice five bed roomed Victorian semi-detached, as it had previously been. Then in 1989 we heard about a five bed roomed detached house which was for sale in Angmering-on-Sea. Although it was in a fairly dilapidated condition our broker thought it would be a good investment, especially as Richard's building business was expanding at the time, so we decided to buy the house in Angmering-on-Sea and sell our house in Worthing. For a time we needed to keep possession of both houses while alterations were carried out on our new property, but then when we tried to sell the Worthing house, we couldn't find a buyer, so we found tenants to live in it – but what they were paying us didn't even cover our mortgage payments! In the end the need to put both properties up for sale became overwhelming as Richard's business started to develop serious financial problems. The house that we were living in was sold for cash after I had asked God to help, but the other property in Worthing was re-possessed by the mortgage company when Richard's business went bankrupt.

To those looking on it must have seemed such a mess, but we both knew that God was sorting things out, just as we had asked Him too, by reversing all our wrong financial moves. We had after all given Him carte blanche to do what He liked with the business and our possessions and He surely did that! Because we both knew it was the Lord working in our lives, we had a tremendous sense of relief that something was going on which was outside our control, but within His. Friends and acquaintances, however who were not Christians were puzzled by our reaction to what seemed like total financial ruin, and teasingly referred to us as the happiest bankrupts they knew!

Shortly after Richard came to know the Lord we formed Escape as a Christian ministry with the purpose of helping the Christian community come to a greater understanding of cult members and how to reach out to them in love. We began to operate a help line and we became more and more aware that there was a very great need in the community at large outside the churches for information and advice. The name Escape came during a prayer time that we had together in 1992. We were moved by the words of Psalm 124 and especially verse 7

We are like a bird escaped from the snare of the fowlers; the snare is broken and we have escaped.

We also saw a great need in the Christian community for more understanding of cult members who were lost in the darkness into which involvement in destructive organisations took them. We wanted to help them through the sharing of our testimony and our growing knowledge of mind control techniques. We thought we would be mainly involved in speaking to churches or their leaders to help inform and warn them about the dangers that Christians and non-believers could unwittingly fall into. But as soon as we set up the help line the floodgates opened and we were inundated with calls from families and friends of active members of different cults as well the media, the social and health services and the police. It was and has continued to be our policy never to solicit attention to the ministry, but only to respond to inquiries. In spite of strictly adhering to that policy we have now spoken to many hundreds of families and friends with loved ones who have been involved in Scientology as well as ex-members, and active members of the organisation who have seen the Web pages outlining our work. But the feeling that the Lord wanted us to become even more involved was growing, and supported by various events not least of all by a conversation I had with the leader of a local church, following a talk I had given to his church.

'You know Bonnie, I still can't help feeling that if you were to come and live in East Grinstead, you would be so much more available to the churches here to help them deal with the threat of Scientology'.

I didn't quite know what to make of the statement that this local church leader had made to me – again. The fact was that this idea was the last thing I wanted to contemplate. In Scientology circles East Grinstead had for some considerable time been thought of as the International Headquarters. In fact when Hubbard was living in the Manor, it was known as the World Wide Headquarters and at any given time there would be hundreds of Scientology members, English and European, living in close proximity to 'the Castle' as it is called. I was adamant that I would never live there as I couldn't think of a less desirable place to be than in close proximity to so many people who would misunderstand and no doubt be hostile to what we were trying to do.

I has spent enough time visiting Jon to know that he was constantly at risk from the Intelligence Department of Scientology – known as the Office of Special Affairs – and living at such close quarters to them just made their job that much easier. So, East Grinstead was the last place I ever wanted to end up living. But it will come as no surprise to anyone who has done business with God that He had another plan in mind!

Gradually we were persuaded that this was the Lord's next move for us and we eventually moved to East Grinstead in March 1993. We started to rent the property of a couple in our church fellowship who had decided to move to the USA for six months. It was a modern, tastefully decorated terrace house, conveniently located only minutes from the town centre.

Just a month after we moved to East Grinstead, in April to be precise, the Scientologists opened a bookstore and Personality Testing Centre in the High Street. This disturbed the local Christian community who felt that the people in the area, especially High School students were now at risk by the increased profile and information that would stem from the High Street store. The local clergy wrote a letter of warning to the community at large and had it published in the local paper. Then a group of about forty Christians decided to have a prayer vigil outside the shop on the 17th of May. They asked us if they could distribute our leaflet What The Scientologists Don't Tell You and they handed out about 500 copies.

I am sure that many of the people who visit East Grinstead to shop or view the timber-framed houses have no idea of the spiritual activity within its boundaries. The town is renowned for the original Tudor buildings which adorn the High Street and it's a delight to spend time visiting the shops there.

But apart from the appealing architecture it has the peculiar reputation in some circles as being the 'cult' capital of Europe. It's an interesting fact that there are several headquarters of international organisations within in a short radius of the town. The London temple of the Mormons is close by. The Jehovah's Witnesses have a large branch. The neighbouring village of Forest Row is the home of the Anthroposophists, a group influenced greatly by the writings of Rudolph Steiner. The Pagan Federation has an active membership and there is speculation that there are several active Wicca covens who meet in Ashdown Forest. And of course Scientology has its international headquarters at

Saint Hill with a castle built by Hubbard to house the Administrative Offices and Course rooms, as well as The Manor, his baronial home. Whether or not each of these groups would willingly accept the title of 'cult' is a matter for conjecture I suppose, but a TV documentary a few years ago looked at the high number of new religious movements that had chosen East Grinstead as their headquarters and asked the question, 'Why East Grinstead?'

So we found ourselves relocated in a place we believed was of God's choosing for us. But from the day we arrived I felt distinctly uncomfortable spiritually, in spite of the fact that I had no particular reason naturally to think that way. We belonged to a loving local church fellowship and were welcomed by members of several of the local churches. The uneasiness I felt was soon to be explained as we were on the brink of what I call our 'Job' experience, who Bible students will recall that Job went through a series of traumatic and testing experiences.

I was to learn the very valuable lesson of making God my stronghold in time of trouble, finding afresh that He is my Rock and Hiding place when everything around is uncertain.

Chapter Nine

On Eagles Wings

As I switched on the TV to find out about the latest escapades of the characters who live in Coronation Street, Britain's longest running soap opera, I had a twinge of guilt. It was a lovely balmy summers evening – far too nice to spend in front of the box. 'We should all be out enjoying the delights of a picnic in Ashdown Forest,' I thought to myself, 'after all, the times when the climate for that kind of thing in England is right are few and far between'.

It was one of those evenings when we all knew what would have been fun – but then chose something else to do anyway! When I told Richard I wanted to stay home and take it easy for the evening, he said he would go to a house group meeting which was run by members of our church, just a five minute car ride away. I was pleased in more ways than one at his decision. I was glad that he wanted to have fellowship with other Christians, without feeling that I should always be there too, and happy that he felt relaxed enough to leave me in the house without him, as I knew that since the publication of the Hate Campaigner leaflet by the Scientologists, he had been reluctant to leave me and the girls on our own.

I found the Coronation Street programme fascinating, as

I did all types of television programs which depicted English life real, or imagined. But after just a few minutes into the first half of the programme there was a knock on the front door. I guessed that it would be one of the girls' friends, trying to entice them outside for a game before it went dark. Then I heard Desi say 'Wait here, I'll get my mother'. That struck me as unusual as most of the people who called to see us were friends who would naturally be invited in.

Everything from that point on happened quite quickly. I looked over the back of my chair to see a woman whose name I knew to be Sheila walking down the hallway with a man called Graeme. She was calling my name as she walked down the passage. She was a Scientologist, and head of their Office of Special Affairs. Graeme was also from that same office. I recognised them because they had been main players in the distribution of the Hate Campaigner leaflet a few weeks earlier.

The house we were renting at the time was tiny. Richard and I used to refer to it as the Barbie and Ken house. So, in spite of the fact that these two intruders were already walking down the passage I was still able to block them from entering the lounge – indicating just how quickly I could move when stirred!

Before they had time to enter into any kind of dialogue I insisted in no uncertain terms that they leave my home immediately, and after repeating my demand three or four times, they walked back to the front door, as the speed with which I moved towards them mad them back down my front hallway and out the front door. I was probably as shocked as they were by my reaction. But then I can be fairly fierce where my family's apparent safety are concerned, and I had made the point quite clearly in my encounters with them on the street that I wanted my children left out of our disagreements. So that evening I wasn't willing to enter into any discussions with them while the girls were present, and their arrival was unannounced and uninvited. I made these points quite clear as we all moved towards the front door.

'Sorry Mum, I didn't invite them in – they waited 'til I turned my back and just came in anyway' said Desi, looking shaken. 'That's OK honey, you did what was right – and don't worry, I don't think they'll be back', I said trying to sound confident, but feeling pretty shaken myself.

The drama of which we had just been a part of was far more action packed than anything that Coronation Street was currently offering. I still find it puzzling that they chose to visit on an evening when Richard had just gone out. It was an unusual occurrence for him to leave us for any reason, especially in the evenings.

I tried to act and sound relaxed, for the sake of the girls, but the fact was the incident would change the way that we would operate as a family from then on. Up to that point we extended a warm welcome to all who visited us – believing hospitality to be a hallmark of Christian living. After that we learnt to be guarded and wary when we heard a knock at the door, and for several years after the girls didn't rush to be the first to answer when a visitor called at the house or the phone started to ring. In fact, even now Richard is always the one to answer both the door and the phone if he is at home when people call.

From a legal point of view there was nothing I could have really reported to the police, even if I had been that way inclined. What would I have told them? That two people had walked into my home, after knocking at the door, and waiting while I was called? Hardly a major crime! Yet I knew the reason they had come round to see me in the manner in which they had was to let me know that they could bring their grievances to my front room any time they wanted to – whether I liked it or not.

My feelings were confirmed when I saw for the first time one of their major publications, euphemistically entitled The Freedom Newspaper, which Scientology would use to write about me and the family over the next few years. And they were not just some short paragraphs tucked away on page 13! They were glossy, expensive, magazine style pieces that were distributed throughout England, and sent to all sections of the media, and to anyone else they felt they could reach who had any contact with us.

I'll never forget the first time I opened a copy and saw a colour photograph of myself and Richard staring back at me, and backing up the endless lines of text with the attention grabbing headline Escape Couple Escapes Creditors, a reference to Richard's failed business venture, which of course he did everything to prevent. After all, who in their right mind would want to be made bankrupt?

In spite of all that I had gone through to that point, life had not prepared me for the stomach- wrenching feeling that hit me when I started to read what they had written, knowing that thousands of others would be reading it too, without knowing our side of the story. What I did begin to find was that this and other incidents started to push me further into God, and I took comfort from Psalm 32 where it says in verse seven:

'Thou art a hiding-place for me, From distress Thou dost keep me, With songs of deliverance thou dost compass me.'

God started to become a real Hiding Place for me, and has continued to be ever since. I also had the comfort of knowing that Jesus understood completely what I was going through and feeling. I was able to find an incredible peace of mind in the eye of what was to become a hurricane of lies and innuendo the Scientologists would publish about us both.

The way we got to know about these wretched publications varied. Sometimes they would be sent to us through the mail. At other times Stephen, the vicar of our local parish church, who was a lovely friend of ours, would gently point out that a member of the congregation had been sent a copy of the Freedom newspaper, containing the latest story. At other times I found out what had been published about me whilst shopping in the town when a Christian from a church other than our own would stop and tell me what they had recently read about us.

Around that time God gave us a core group of people who I called Joshuas and Calebs after the two Old Testament characters, who had faith to occupy the Promised Land when the others felt hesitant. Our friends, who were also full of faith, surrounded us with love and prayer and constant encouragement. And boy, did we need that. Especially when we discovered that the Scientology organisation had hired private investigators who spent the next few months interviewing all the creditors of Richard's bankruptcy, in order to build up a case against us.

We had no idea when the whole thing started that the harassment that the Scientologists waged against us would continue for six long years. They demoralised us in a number of ways from videoing us in the street, keeping watch on our house and contacting our friends and neighbours with a view to finding out something about us that would help them portray us in a bad light, thus discrediting the work that we were doing.

Whenever they could they would try to publicly humiliate us. One incident occurred on what was one of Ireland's top chat shows, the Late, Late Show which was skilfully presented by the brilliantly articulate Gay Bryne. For those who never had the good fortune to see the show, it was a mixture of debate, chat and entertainment, similar in some ways to the BBC TV's programme called Wogan, presented by Terry Wogan -also Irish.

Mary Johnson, a lady we had got to know through our counselling work who had ended up a good friend of ours, had been asked to appear on the show together with a family we had been able to help with the problems they had experienced when a member of their family had been won over to the Scientology movement. Peter Mansell, Scientology's public relations representative at the time, was also asked to appear on the show, to represent Scientology's point of view. By this time, Scientology had compiled several packs of information about Richard and myself based on the information unearthed by the various private detectives they had hired. Peter Mansell was well briefed on this material and part of his job was to make this information available to the newspaper reporters and editors and television and radio researchers and presenters who Scientology believed might have contacted me for a statement or invited me to appear on their programmes. He wasted no time in saying that the whole problem was down to one person and their hate campaign. I'll leave you to guess who he was talking about, and how I felt as he launched into me on 'live' TV! A recording of the show was later screened on Channel 4 for the benefit of British viewers.

The decision to make myself available for TV appearances was not taken lightly, as I had to count the cost in terms of the risk it posed to our whole family. But Richard and I prayed about it and decided that I would tell the truth about Scientology as I understood it to be and that we would make ourselves available to the public through an open help-line. We felt that although it might be considered risky in terms of the safety of ourselves or the children, we wanted to set them an example that they must tell the truth about their experiences in the hope that it will protect others from danger.

News travels fast in the world of the media and my name must have started appearing on contact lists. So I was often called by the press and media I found I was quite comfortable talking to them. I haven't been frightened by it but I put that down to God's grace empowering my efforts.

Whenever I am asked to speak or write about my experiences Richard and I always seek God's wisdom in prayer and we have at times refused an interview because we don't feel at peace about it. I know that the media is a powerful tool informing people about the dangers of cult involvement and God has been gracious in sending us divine appointments that are genuine in their presentation of the story of our involvement with Scientology.

There were several incidents when I was appearing on a 'live' TV programme with a member of the Church of Scientology and I suddenly found myself under personal attack. But when the President of the Church of Scientology started to make allegations about my character on the Richard and Judy Show, the former jumped to my defence and asked why I was being attacked in such a personal way. The Scientology representative should have known better. Englishmen can sometimes appear quiet and unassuming, but I've always found that they will jump to the defence of the underdog, and will always come to the aid of a woman under attack. And I also know that without the support of our Christian brothers and sisters we would have never endured. They were a constant source of encouragement to us through their prayer and practical help, and the love they showed to us through it all.

One such group called themselves WIGS (Women's Intercessory Group).They were like an army of spiritual prayer warriors who built a hedge of protection around us so that the worst of the attacks that were ranged against us never even penetrated. June, who was the unofficial leader of the group, and Tim her husband became like spiritual parents to us both, which was appropriate as both our natural parents had died before all the hassle started, which I am sure was in God's plan as they would have worried and fretted about what we were having to endure. But in Tim and June we were given spiritual parents who hugged us and wiped away our tears, which came in floods at times.

It was around this time we decided that we must do something other than pray, concerning the harassment that seemed to be occurring on an increasingly frequent basis, and the totally untrue statements that they had made about me in the Hate Campaigner leaflet.

We knew of course that we wouldn't just be fighting for the injustices that had been meted out towards us, but for all those families with whom we had come into contact or we had read about who needed someone to stand up for them, who maybe didn't have the security of knowing as we knew that we were safe and secure, and in the palm of God's Almighty Hand. We became convinced that if we could manage to bring the injustices we knew about that were happening to families and members of Scientology on a daily basis to the attention of the judicial system then others would be strengthened by our resolve. The more concentrated Scientology's efforts became to limit our freedom to speak, the more real issues became clear.

These were the times when Richard and I clung to scriptures that spoke of the everlasting mercy and grace of God, and that Jesus had paid the price of our shame by his death on the Cross. One verse was of particular comfort:

I have loved you,my people with an everlasting love. With unfailing love I have drawn you to myself.' Jeremiah 31.3

If we naturally felt hurt and upset by what Scientology printed about us, we also knew that we served a God who loved us first, unconditionally, and without reservation or limit. I am one of those people who talks to Jesus as if He were sitting next to me because I believe He is and I believe He knows me so well that it isn't necessary to be super-spiritual about how I feel. I just pour out my fear and pain to Him and He listens quietly. And sometimes He speaks to me in words of scripture like this one in Isaiah:

Come now, and let us reason together. Though your sins are like scarlet, they shall be as white as snow: though they are red like crimson, they shall be like wool. (Isa.1:18)

I was able to come to the understanding that my place in God's family had been purchased for a great price and my standing with Him was not dependent on my personal clean slate, but on His.

It's funny but the greater the vilification of our personal reputation the more we were strengthened by the knowledge that long before those Scientology articles had been written, we had been accepted and loved by God. We had come to Him just as we were and we had been forgiven for all our sins.

But sometimes it is comforting to have someone you can pick up the phone and call knowing that you have a earthly pastor who will listen to you, and someone who you never doubt will do whatever he can to help you. In every Christian Fellowship we have attended, we have been greatly blessed with just such a person, learning something important from each one. And although some Christians spend their whole lives in one denominational group, because we moved around, and got involved in various situations, we became familiar with various types of service and came to appreciate and love the different styles of worship that make up the Christian church in the Western world, realising that they express different aspects of God's character and care.

When we first moved to East Grinstead we attended a house church called Hosanna, where we learned to be free in expressing our love of God, and where we were hungry to understand God's Word more fully. We knew that Jim, our pastor loved us and was keen to keep us safe. Then after about a year we felt it was right to move to a little Anglican church, called St. John's in Felbridge. We were further sheltered from the storms there, as we carried on with the work of Escape, and learned more about the ways of God. We felt protected by God as He 'bore us on eagle's wings and brought us to Himself' (Exodus 19.4)

The vicar of that church was a man called Stephen, who was one of the most remarkable preachers of the gospel I have ever come across, as well as being a person of extraordinarily quiet courage. He got involved in several daring exploits that we were dealing with, and he tempered our impulsiveness with much wisdom. The way he pitched in when we were trying to help a man called Nowell is a good example.

Nowell was an African who had parted company from the Scientologists at Saint Hill, and had subsequently sought our help in dealing with the results of being involved for a period of time with Scientology. One of Nowell's concerns was based on a very practical fact – the Scientology organisation still held his passport. He requested our help in getting it back for him. Richard and I knew that we would have to physically visit Saint Hill if the passport was to be retrieved, and on the spur of the moment we asked Stephen to accompany us. To our delight and without a moment's hesitation he agreed to do so. Soon Richard and I, together with Stephen and Nowell, were on a passport rescue mission, not knowing quite what kind of reception we would receive.

As we approached the front doors of the castle we were surrounded with security guards and were photographed and videoed continually. One irate staff member confronted Stephen angrily with the question, 'Are you from that Born-again Church?' 'My dear', he gently replied, 'Do you know what it means to be born again'?

He asked her to sit down on a low wall nearby and then I heard him begin 'There was a man called Nicodemus who came to ask Jesus that question............'

I don't know how much of the story she heard but I noticed she walked quietly away a few minutes later. That tranquil scene only lasted a short while as those in charge at Saint Hill had called the police to force us to leave. They pretended to search for Nowell's passport and after a fairly long delay we realised that they had no intention of giving us the passport but had in fact called the police to arrest Nowell on trumped up criminal charges which were later dropped. But at that point the police had no alternative but to arrest him, taking him away in a police car. But before we were able to get into a car to follow Nowell another woman staff member approached Stephen, angrily waving a letter which she had in some way got hold of. It was a letter that Stephen had written to the local newspaper a few days before with a view to warning the people of the town about the Scientology bookshop. She told him in no uncertain terms that he was not welcome there and Stephen was escorted off the property. But all was not lost. The police officers who had been called to the scene were able to get Nowell's passport released to them, which meant that our main objective had been achieved. But not without cost. Within five minutes of Stephen being escorted off the property we also received the same unfriendly treatment.

This is a wonderful example of the kind of courage our pastors showed when God placed us in their care. I call them my Joshuas and Calebs and we have had many. Each was particularly suited to meet the need for pastoral care we had in those long years.

Charlie Crane was out of the same mould as Stephen. Also from London, he was full of the straight talking forthrightness that I understand far better than the convoluted, polite, carefully constructed advice that some ministers choose to dole out to their flock. We got to know him when our youngest daughter Andreanna had joined the Girls Brigade that Charlie's church, Trinity Methodist, ran and we were invited to a family service to see their parade.

We immediately felt at home with the Churches' free and enthusiastic worship style. Although I am not comfortable with denominational labels I could probably be described as a Pentecostal and I missed that style of worship. And so we eventually joined Trinity Church. But by this time we were a bit wary of joining any church group or Christian fellowship before we had given them a full briefing about the work that we were doing via Escape, and the probable consequences to them from the Scientology movement. Obviously its not every minister's cup of tea to have a Private Investigator knocking at the door! So I made an appointment to see Charlie not just to let him know everything that was happening but to ask him for guidance as to how to go forward with our work. We had a wonderful time of sharing and prayer and I knew I could open my heart to him and he would help me to understand more about the biblical principles we were striving to live by.

I have noticed that often people in full time ministry struggle with difficulties and trials that seem to centre around their families. We had a fair share of these trials and Charlie was someone we could call on who would give us practical help as well as spiritual advice. As the years passed and the intensity of the Scientology reaction to our work grew, Charlie was always only a few minutes away and his door was always open.

Now we had to brace ourselves for all that would ensue as we sought to bring a libel action against the Scientology movement, which was after all a huge international organisation with millions of dollars at its disposal. This course of action would bring new and valued friends into our lives who would show us depths of courage and commitment we had not encountered before.

The first person to recognise our need for legal protection was a very brave friend of ours called Beverley. We first got to know her when she provided accommodation for one of the Africans who had left Saint Hill. She knew the importance of getting good legal advice for him, and others like him in regard to the issues surrounding their entry and stay in this country.

The first time we met her Beverley offered legal advice if we should ever need it. We felt moved by this generous and spontaneous act. It was rare for people to volunteer to help us, and we felt blessed that we had a deeply committed Christian solicitor willing to represent us. So when Scientology first distributed the Hate Campaigner leaflet, we were confident she would know what to do.

When she heard that we wanted to go ahead with our libel

action she suggested we meet a barrister in London. He was not at all what he expected. Richard mentioned to me on the way home that he felt he had more than a marked resemblance to Michael Caine! That fact had escaped me, even if it were true. I was trying to come to terms with the one and only question he fired at me. Looking me straight in the eye he said, without emotion 'Could you tell me, what incident in your past would you be most concerned that Scientology might discover and expose?'

As those words were spoken, as well as trying to think of all the things I had done in my life which might suddenly become public knowledge, I began to realise the personal cost and consequences of getting involved in a libel action. But on the other hand I had never thought about the legal action we took as being specifically for me, but hoped I would be the voice for countless ex-members to protest about their treatment at the hands of this organisation because they had chosen to speak out. People like Lisa McPherson who may have died during a seventeen-day stay at the Scientology Headquarters in Clearwater, Florida. Hardly a day went by when I didn't think and pray about her and her family. I knew that they were just some of many who had suffered at the hands of the Scientology movement, by losing a family member through separation or death. I also knew that I needed to speak the truth about Scientology as I understood it to be. I believed it needed to be proclaimed so that the captives could be set free, the prisoners released and the broken hearted could become whole again. I felt a commitment to warn others of the dangers of that organisation and I was not ashamed of what I felt called to do.

As it turned out our relationship with the Michael Caine look- alike barrister was short lived. On our second visit to

London to talk about our libel action against the Church of Scientology Beverley met us at Victoria Station and told us there had been a change of plan.

'You've been referred to other chambers', she said, trying to make herself heard above the noise of a train leaving the station, and a platform announcement. 'They are very good,' she continued, 'and are considered to be libel specialists. You'll be under the care of a lady called Alex'.

'Thanks Beverley for everything that you're doing for us,' I said, grateful that I didn't need to raise my voice to reply as the train had left the station. 'I just feel that if God wants to see this litigation happen everything will be provided, including finance. And I don't believe any man can shut doors that God wants to be open!'

Alex proved to be a perfect choice. As I spent time with her explaining what had happened to us in the past I began to realise that we had someone working with us who really understood why we were so determined to bring our case into the legal arena. But she didn't hold out any false hopes. She explained the difficulties of bringing a libel action in Britain, and that apart from the fact that it was very expensive other things would be needed in vast quantities: guts, stamina and a single-minded approach, as well as patience. She also reminded us that legal actions of this type can drag on for years. Legal aid was something that would not be available, so all expenses would have to be borne by us, meaning that if we ran out of money part way through we would not be able to bring the action to trial.

But after doing her duty by telling us those sobering facts, she did conclude by saying she felt we had a good case, and, if we had the stomach for it, we would be successful!

A few days later Beverley called to say Alex had offered

to represent us without charge. English Law as it then stood had no facility for what is known as pro bono representation, which meant that Alex wouldn't receive any of her costs. Her gift to us of her time and skills would prove to be huge, and none of us then could have known just how big a commitment that would be. Beverley also came on board that day too, and our legal battle was ready to commence. But this battle would prove to be neither short nor straightforward, with many twists and turns. And a new battle was just around the corner, engineered by the Scientology organisation, needless to say.

Chapter Ten

A Judgement of Solomon

I know that Beverley's decision to help us was not taken lightly, especially as it meant that she would be receiving no financial remuneration from us. The same applied to Alex. And although they were not receiving any payment, they themselves paid dearly for the work they started to do on our behalf. Because they were helping us, they automatically became enemies in the eyes of the Scientologists. And over the next two years odd things started to happen to Beverley. She would be followed home. People would sit outside her home, and trail her when she left. Others went through her dustbin to try to retrieve documents that she had thrown away which might be useful to them, and on one horrific occasion a car which had been parked outside her house drove towards her in what appeared to be an attempt to run her over. Eventually the pressure of these events proved too much.

One night just as we had finished our evening meal, the phone rang. As always, Richard dashed into the hall to take the call. He was surprised to find himself talking to Beverley's husband Mike, someone with whom we had little contact, as virtually all of our dealings had been with Bev. Although Mike speaks in a soft-spoken voice, Richard detected a tension the moment he began to talk.

'Hello Richard, this is Mike here, Beverley's husband. I'm calling to talk to you about Bev. She's not doing so well, mainly because of the case, and I would like you to release her from her legal obligations with you. It's affecting her health you see – physically and mentally.'

This news was a real shock and came right out of the blue. We suspected that Bev and her family were being watched and there was great interest in any documents she may have discarded.. She had also had a late night visit from the police accompanied by a Scientology member who had claimed, falsely of course, that she holding stolen documents in the office she had in her home. Although all these incidents were obviously unpleasant for her we thought at the time that she dealt with them all pretty well.

Mike continued with his message, in a polite but firm voice by saying, 'This has got to end'.

'Of course Mike. I'll talk to Bonnie and get back to you as soon as possible, said Richard, sorry to hear that the suspected, accumulated, harassment had finally taken its toll on her.

We realised that Beverley must be at a complete end of herself, to have allowed Mike to make the call to us. We knew her to be a strong person, very sure of her legal standing and ability, a strong Christian that we had prayed with and grown to love very much. We moved swiftly to get her off the case, our actions coming into effect within 24 hours or so of the phone call.

However, one of the first repercussions of Beverley coming off our case was that Alex no longer had a solicitor to instruct her, and so she also finished working on our behalf.

A little while before all this happened Beverley told us

that Scientology had filed a counter-claim in response to my writ alleging that I had libelled them by handing out the leaflet What the Scientologists Don't Tell You. I responded by asserting that the leaflet was true and contained fair criticism of Scientology. We then learnt that we were being sued by Narcanon – a so-called drug rehabilitation programme sponsored by members of Scientology. They were suing us for the description of the Narcanon programme as contained in the booklet we distributed called The Total Freedom Trap. If that wasn't enough in 1996 Scientology brought another action against Richard and me, this time for handing out another leaflet about them in connection with The Big Story – a documentary about Scientology produced by 20/20 Television. Although many other people also handed out copies of this leaflet, no one other than us was sued by Scientology.

Just like water which starts out as a small stream, and as more water is added to it turns into a torrent, threatening to flood everywhere it goes, so we were engulfed by claims and counter claims that were likely to swamp and overwhelm us. We were now representing ourselves in the libel action we had brought against Scientology. We were also defending their counter-claim, as well as defending the libel action they had brought against us regarding The Big Story leaflet, and the libel action that Narcanon had instigated.

Richard and I were at a loss to know how to deal with all the legal paperwork that was coming our way. We found ourselves totally out of our depth. Then we managed to find a couple of books from the local library which gave us a few pointers on how to proceed, but armed with the might and incredible wealth of the Scientology movement, it really was a David and Goliath situation we were now involved in. Even the thought of entering the Law Courts was daunting.

The first time I saw the Royal Courts of Justice I was struck by their architectural beauty despite the fact that in the months to come I would always associate visiting them with a sinking feeling in my stomach at the thought of yet another hearing. We could never have begun to understand at the beginning of our time as litigants in person how completely exhausting physically and emotionally we would find the whole legal process.

The Law Court buildings looked as though they had been standing there for centuries – an awesome thought to an American like myself whose culture is so much more recent than that of the 'Old Country'. It wasn't hard to imagine men in frock coats and women in long Victorian dresses going up and down the steps, or of major legal battles being fought where passions were raised, and high drama was the order of the day. I knew that some of the finest legal minds stalked these corridors, whose knowledge far exceeded anything Richard and I could ever begin to muster between us. The very thought of even trying made me feel hot and cold at the same time! Then the peace of the Holy Spirit would begin to challenge my negative thoughts, and I remembered afresh that it was God was leading and directing us, and we just needed to trust Him every step of the way.

We relied heavily on the two legal texts we had borrowed from the library. One was a book on libel by Carter-Ruck and the other was a text about discovering evidence written by a barrister called Hodge Malek. I had chosen that one because I knew that Malek had represented Scientology in other cases and I thought it might help us to understand any strategy they might have in mind. Having waded through it a couple of times, I was impressed by the obvious skill and intelligence of the author, and when I discovered that he was to be the Barrister that Scientology would be using against me, I knew that he would be a worthy opponent.

The day before the hearing was due to commence, Richard and I were sat outside the master's chambers, feeling quite nervous and out of place in such awesome surroundings, when we suddenly became aware of a small group of people walking towards us, led by a distinguished man in a very well tailored and probably highly expensive suit. Instead of sweeping past us, as I imagined they would, the group stopped where we were sitting, and the distinguished stranger with a slightly continental air about him began to speak to me.

'Hello – are you Mrs. Woods?' he said. Nodding in surprise that he knew my name, he continued. 'I'm Hodge Malek and I would like to give you a copy of the arguments that I intend to use in the case today.'

'Mr Malek thank you' I said, jumping to my feet. 'I've read your book – twice – and found it fascinating.' He nodded in apparent surprise and waited for my next sentence. But I was now desperately trying to think of something intelligent to say. I couldn't just stand and gawp at him like a goldfish in a bowl! Suddenly, I recalled something in his very detailed and technical book that had puzzled me. I launched in again.

'But I'm intrigued as to why you didn't refer more to Bray, which is after all a very old law text. Was there a particular reason?'

From somewhere in the recesses of my mind I had managed to pull out something that he had written which I could ask an intelligent question .

It was now his turn to look perplexed. He couldn't have known that I had been reading in the law library on the Discovery of Evidence, and had picked up on this particular text which seemed to be one that was often quoted in libel cases. That started a fairly deep and certainly from my point of view interesting conversation when I guess we were both trying to get the measure of each other.

Hodge Malek was handsome, and immaculately dressed. it soon became obvious that he had a razor sharp mind, which had equipped him well for the legal arena. I was later to discover in the Court room that he presented my alleged transgressions so eloquently that even I might have been convinced of them, if I hadn't known better! He had an amazing command of the English language, and our conversation was respectful of each other and animated, and somehow it turned towards God.

'Mrs. Woods, it is evident that you serve a living God , he said with genuine sincerity in his voice. 'But you know' he continued as he made a move to leave 'this is a very difficult case we have both got ourselves involved in, and with all due respect, you would really benefit from being represented by a good law firm'. I smiled, wondering how on earth that could ever be. I was glad to make his acquaintance, and felt that any contest I had with him would be just and honourable.

Although of course I was grateful he had given me a list of the arguments that he intended to use, he was not treating me differently from any other opponent he would be up against. Legal Procedure dictates that the opposing party gives the other party an outline of the arguments that are going to be made at least 24 hours before the hearing so they can construct a response. Then when they are put before the master that is the outline that is followed. When we had a chance to read through what we had been handed we were quite frankly mystified! Couched as they were in legal language, they were very difficult to follow, and even more difficult to defend! I am quite sure it was only through the power of the Holy Spirit that we were able to mount any kind of defence, in the light of all that was coming against us.

Sometimes during a hearing I would be so frightened that my tonsils would feel frozen and I couldn't even speak. My favourite name for the Holy Spirit is The Advocate and it was at these highly vulnerable times that He would show up to represent me. Once the master himself said to Mr. Malek "If Mrs. Woods were to be represented by Counsel this is the advice he would give her," and the master proceeded to clarify for me a legal decision I could make at the time. The very next day Richard and I resolved to start a crash course in understanding the law which would take several super-natural turns in the days to follow.

I began to frequent the chambers of the "practice" master once I discovered it was permissible to come at certain hours and ask questions of whatever master was on duty about procedures. I'm sure my list of questions were ones that were unique in many ways but I found that I was always treated with great respect and understanding by everyone I encountered at the courts. The clerks and secretaries helped me understand the myriad of forms that had to be filed. I started to visit the law library adjoining the courts and read all kinds of legal texts, including those published in earlier centuries. I have a great love of English Literature and I am very much at home with reading the Authorized Version of the Bible and I found the language of one of the texts about evidence familiar.

But it must be said that this ability to read and understand the principles of English Law which we needed to survive this struggle came from God's grace and mercy in response to my predicament. He equipped us in so many ways to face the battle. Richard has always been gifted in writing letters to families and dealing with all the correspondence that we received as a ministry but now he was to face the challenge of writing our legal defence to the various actions Scientology brought against us. As I was named as the plaintiff in the main action I would have to speak in the hearings and so I knew I would need to learn the script of the defence he would prepare and file with the master before the hearing.

Scientology's barrister would prepare arguments that we would only receive 24 hours before the hearings or sometimes they would be handed to us as we walked through the door on the day itself.

Because of the work we had started which involved counselling ex-members of the Scientology movement and their families we had by this time been approached for advice by several hundred families. Scientology had requested that we put into evidence their correspondence from families we had been helping over the years. We were adamant from the outset that their identities should be protected. When we received a decision from the master that supported our viewpoint Scientology began the process which was open to them of lodging an appeal against this decision with a judge in a higher court, and we were therefore summoned to appear in his courtroom.

The day before that happened we travelled to London to collect their barrister's arguments so that I could read about the legal cases he would refer to in the law library. Richard thought it might calm my nerves to be familiar with the surroundings I would be in, so we wandered through the long corridors trying to find the courtroom. Eventually we did locate the correct door only to discover that we had got there a few minutes after the doors were locked for the evening which meant that we couldn't take a look inside.

But then a friendly clerk offered to open it up for us anyway. I found myself walking into this silent and awesome courtroom, the atmosphere heavy with history and all the dramas that had been played out there down the years.

Before me stretched a huge chamber with a dais where the judge sat and rows and rows of seats with higher pedestals scattered about. Suddenly the enormity of what we were due to face began to hit home – and I burst into tears! Thanking the bemused clerk for his kindness through my sobs, we hurriedly left the courts and walked along the Thames for an hour until I calmed down. I found that the gentle flow of the river, and ordinary Londoners and tourists getting on with their day allowed me once again to put things into perspective, even though the challenge in front of us was gigantic.

I wish I could say that I was extraordinarily brave during the following days and months, but that would just not be true. In fact I was more than stroppy in my conversations with God about the decisions we had made. There were many times I wanted to give up but I knew that if I did, the truth as I understood it would be buried under all the legal procedure and the story of the suffering that members like me had endured would never be heard.

We have a dear friend called Ron, a former long-term member of Scientology who had been involved in litigation with them for years and who offered to help us prepare the case. Everyone should know at least one person like Ron! Very much an Englishman, we discovered that he had a kind and calming personality, which immediately put others around him at their ease. He was in his early fifties when we first got to know him, and although he didn't have any Christian beliefs as far as I could make out, he showed so much Christian care and concern in the way that he helped us, displaying great unselfishness, that I often thought what a wonderful follower of Jesus he would make! He would come once or twice a week to help compose our responses to the ever-increasing flood of demands for evidence in the four cases we were now facing, sitting at the desk, occasionally brushing a strand of his light brown hair out of his eyes as he concentrated on the task before him. He was well prepared for all of that, having acquired an 'A' level in Law at some time in his past. With his help we were able to find legal references in law libraries and help us organise the evidence that we would use at trial. At one point we had to allow Scientology to come to inspect the evidence that we planned to use at the trial. Our dear friend Tim had arranged for us to use a room in the city offices so that we didn't have to have the inspection in our home. Ron stayed with us that day, and sat with us while we let the Scientology solicitor and their legal representatives inspect the documentation. Ron was great at organising material and composing a response to a question. He was able to take a mountain of requests and analyse them to see how we could respond to each part. But more importantly he would encourage me to attend just one more hearing and the one became ten and before I knew it, the ten turned into twenty. Ron certainly knew how to encourage – a gift which was invaluable, because at times it seemed as though Richard and I were hitting the depths of despair at all that was coming against us.

Richard became a frequent user of the ancient computer that we had bought years before. Having said that, neither of us were computer whiz kids, and occasionally text would go missing, or other strange things would happen, making us think that maybe it had a mind – and a life force – of its own! In truth, Richard tended to use the computer like a glorified word processor. It was a bit of a dinosaur as far as computers go, and we didn't even know how to back up the work we had created on it. So, instead of saving letters and other electronically generated documents onto a floppy disk, or directly on to the computer's internal memory system, we had to print out a paper copy of everything we produced! We finished up with thirty large storage boxes of documents packed into every corner of our house! In the end Richard had to erect a garden shed, just so that we would have enough storage space for it all.

Finally the day of the appeal arrived, and as we entered the courtroom I asked Mr. Malek how he planned to address the judge. He said that he would address him as 'My Lord'. Now this presented a problem to me. I just couldn't bring myself to address any man in the same terms that I addressed Jesus! I had faced a similar hurdle when addressing the master in chambers and I had been able to use 'Sir'. In the end I decided to call the judge, Your Honour and when I addressed him with that title during the hearing it was always met with a broad smile.

We were directed to a table on the floor of the courtroom while Mr. Malek assumed a position on a rather higher pedestal a good deal away on the other side of the room. I found that a great relief for some reason as it made me less nervous than the close quarters of the master's chambers.

A door opened to the rear of the Judges' high bench and the clerk announced the presence of Justice Scott-Baker. Then the hearing commenced. As usual Richard quietly prayed as I endeavoured to understand how I could respond to this demand for me to reveal the names of the families we had helped, something I was prepared to resist to the point where I might be jailed for contempt if it was ordered.

What got me through was the mental picture I had of

Jesus before His accusers and the obviously cynical and rhetorical question posed by Pontius Pilate: 'What is Truth?'

I had prepared an urgent request to the judge to deny their request and when he asked for my response to Mr. Malek's argument I asked if I might read my statement that was scribbled on a bit of paper. The judge was more than gracious as I should have submitted it as part of my affidavit, and he transcribed himself what I said about my fears of what would happen to these families if their names were known to the organisation. He would later rule that although the content of the letters would have to be given to the court, the identifying details of those who had written them could be blanked out so they could not be recognized. Truly a judgment of Solomon's standard. Our prayers had been answered once again!

Although we were doing all that we could to handle the legal manoeuvres in which we had got involved, fellow Christians and in fact all our friends were concerned for us and many began to realise, as we did, that we urgently needed some professional help, just as Hodge Malek had suggested some time before.

We had many friends who made inquiries everywhere they could think of to try to acquire some legal help for us. One particular friend called Dave, had suggested that we contact Liberty, an organization that is concerned with the protection of freedom of speech. We first made contact with Dave via the Internet. We discovered that he and his friends felt strongly about the right of every individual to exercise free speech and would demonstrate outside Scientology offices on a regular basis to protest against what they considered to be Scientology's violation of human rights and civil liberties. He seemed to know about the legal avenues open to us, so when he suggested we contacted Liberty we wrote to their legal department. About a month later we received a reply saying they were not able to help us directly, but asking if we would like them to refer our case to the Liberty panel? Formerly the National Council for Civil Liberties, it was founded by journalist Ronald Kidd, after he witnessed the use of police agents provocateurs inciting violence during the hunger marches in London in November 1932. We didn't discover until much later who the Liberty panel were but we immediately said yes as we were always open to any suggestion that might offer us some legal expertise.

Then a letter arrived in the post in May that would restore my faith in the idea that any mail through the door could be good! Ripping open the letter, I saw that the stationery was headed 'Allen and Overy' and it gave their address as One New Change. The letter said they were solicitors who would consider helping us with our legal battle. But my mind wasn't on the content of the letter so much as the odd address. One New Change! What kind of address was that, I wondered to myself? I stared at it again. It didn't sound like any London address I had ever heard of. I somehow got the idea that perhaps we had been sent this letter as a kind of cruel joke and I decided to see for myself if such law offices actually existed. The simplest way would have been to call the phone number at the bottom of the notepaper, but for some reason that just never occurred to me! Instead I carefully folded the letter and tucked it into the pocket of my best jeans and caught the train to London. I had intended to make the journey that day anyway, as I wanted to visit a friend of mine who was being treated at Guys Hospital.

After spending a pleasant time with my friend, who was well on the way to recovery, I wondered how the rest of my time in the capital would turn out. The day was bright and sunny as I left the hospital, in sharp contrast to the mists of doubt that were still swirling around in my mind about the validity of this Law firm with the weird address. 'Could it be for real?' I said to the Lord. I got no definite reply, so thought my only option was to go and hunt it down if I could.

Almost immediately after this brief conversation with the Almighty, I looked up to see a big red London bus with a placard on the front that said 'St. Paul's'. That was significant because someone had said to me that they had a inkling that 'One New Change' was near St. Paul's Cathedral

Now up to this point I had never actually travelled on a bus through London because I was usually with Richard and he always took the Tube. Not that that mode of transport made me feel particularly safe – I had even managed to get lost on the Circle Line when he was with me once! But putting all thoughts of fear to one side, I stuck out my hand to draw the bus driver's attention to me, and to my relief the bus stopped. I walked quickly a few feet ahead of me to where it was now parked.

'One New Change? Yes, I know where that is', the driver said kindly to my inquiry. 'Hop on board, and I'll take you along if you like. I've got to drive there, before I start to pick up fares at St. Paul's – and I'll show you the sights of London, for free if you like!'

So I became the only passenger on a very enjoyable journey across London with the driver pointing out all the major tourist attractions along the way. Before I knew it, the bus came to a halt, and it was time to bid my newfound friend goodbye. As I got off the bus at One New Change – yes it really did exist – I looked up to see an impressive office building that covered an entire city block. I suddenly realised that the letter was not a hoax, and what's more I was now standing outside the building that could just be the answer to my prayers as far as professional help with our legal battle was concerned. Without a second thought I fell to my knees right there on the pavement, giving a prayer of thanksgiving to Jesus – much to the bemusement of the people hurrying by. As I did so I was reminded of the Scripture which says:

Now to him who by the power at work within us is able to do far more abundantly than all that we ask or think (Ephesians 3:20)

A little while later I was face to face with the individual who had written to me a few days before. If I had imagined some elderly gent with grey hair wearing a pinstriped suit, I couldn't have been more wrong. The person handling our case was an elegant lady called Sharon, a woman in her late thirties, with dark hair and a wonderfully warm and friendly smile. We found her to be a truly amazing person, very competent, who totally believed in what we were trying to achieve. She explained that we would be taken on as a 'Liberty' case, as what we were wanting to bring to court involved issues of protection of free speech. She told us that each year a panel made up from the largest law firms in Britain meet to choose which cases they are going to represent – for free. We became one of their favoured cases, which meant that we were treated as private clients. Only those who are familiar with Allen and Overy's London offices will truly appreciate what the Lord had provided for us. This was no back street barrister outfit, but a smart City firm of Lawyers. God was proving once again to be a wonderful provider, and able to give us the very best that money could buy. But then, we knew that we couldn't have a richer benefactor than Him!

A little while after my first meeting with Sharon, Richard, Ron and I were invited back to have lunch with the legal team that would be working on our case, and from that day forward I would always refer to them as the 'A' team!

The meeting took place in a beautiful conference room, where we were introduced to Tim, who headed the team up, as well as various solicitors and trainees, who would be working on our case. Although there was a lot of serious talk to get through, they couldn't help teasing us about the number of people we now had working for us, compared to how it had been before, which was just us – and two borrowed library books!

Although we now had the wonderful help of Allen and Overy it still meant that Richard and I had to invest thousands of hours of work preparing to prove at the trial that the statements about Scientology we had made in our leaflets were true. Literally thousands of documents were prepared and reviewed. Our lawyers had contact with dozens of potential witnesses, whilst Richard and I devoted countless hours to preparing our defence of the actions Scientology had brought against us.

But more drama was to follow as our case went to Court – bringing with it a new and daunting experience where once again God would reveal His love to us.

Chapter Eleven

The Cavalry finally arrives!

I guess I grew up watching too many Cowboys and Indians movies which in later life have started to impact upon the way I see things, because when Allen and Overy took the decision to represent at no cost, it distinctly reminded me of one of those scenes in the Western films when the pioneers are being pursued by a horde of wild Indians – knowing that there is nowhere for them to hide. Then, just as they begin to think that the end is near, they see a cloud of dust forming in the distance across the hills, and as the blue and gold flag of the first rider comes into view they realise their worries are over. The Cavalry has finally arrived!

As Richard and I started to get to know the team at Allen and Overy we could have never guessed that our situation would turn out to be very much like the end of a classic western. But before that was to happen, there were lots of other situations for us to pass through first.

Now that we were being professionally represented by a top London law firm we began to travel to the capital at least once a week to meet with them. They in turn began the arduous task of re-drafting the cases we were involved in. These processes propelled us into a totally different world from anything any of our friends were experiencing. We traded a reasonably normal lifestyle for a legal battleground, and my mind seemed to be constantly crammed with thoughts of affidavits, defence arguments and legal pleas. Our preoccupation with things legal even affected our mode of travel. While friends might hop on a bus or train when visiting London, we took a black cab from the offices of Allen and Overy across the street from St. Paul's to the High Court which is about a ten minute journey, and sometimes two black cabs just to hold all the documents we needed to take with us as well as the legal team usually consisting of two solicitors, a trainee solicitor and other trained staff! As we rushed along city streets on our legal pilgrimage in those famous black taxis which held a special delight for me as an American, I couldn't help wondering at times just what I had got myself into!

We soon discovered that Allen and Overy had assigned a large number of specially trained personnel called paralegals to prepare the documentation for trial. They were very ably led by a man called Vince. What a guy he was! Although I guess he would be described as average in height and build, he was way above average in the help he gave to us. What set him apart was his congeniality. He always made us feel so very welcome, and never failed to patiently answer my thousands of questions. He was brilliant at his job, and we watched in admiration and awe as he carefully organised a veritable mountain of documentation.

Before I got involved with the legal battles that now seem to pervade every part of my life, I was not aware of all the legal procedures that have to be gone through before a trial can take place. 'Hearings', which are known in the legal world as 'interlocutories', are undertaken before any case is heard in Court. These have been devised to iron out any points of law that might be in dispute between the parties before the court case starts – the idea being that this will prevent trial time being taken up with legal discrepancies between the two opposing parties. But, as in any system it can be wrongly used, or in Scientology policy terms 'the law can easily be used to harass!' All told, we must have attended around twenty-five of these Hearings which is a lot higher than the average Court case would normally involve.

A lot of what we were now trying to deal with on a daily basis was in truth way out of our depth. But a wonderful consequence of Allen and Overy taking on our case was that we started to work again with Alex. She had no alternative but to pull out when Bev no longer felt able to represent us, but Allen and Overy approached Alex's chambers once they started to represent us, and asked her to come back and defend us once more. You can imagine how overjoyed we were to be working with her again. But her agreement to get back on the case was at no small cost to her – the vast majority of the work she did for us, amounting to hundreds of hours, was of a voluntary nature, which she did simply because she believed in us, and what we were trying to achieve. People of her calibre are rare indeed!

As we arrived at court for the appeal Hearing Alex introduced us to someone else who would be a key person in our fight for justice. His name was Desmond, a very well respected Queen's Counsel from Alex's chambers who had volunteered to represent us in the Hearing, who looked very distinguished in his black robes and grey wig whenever he appeared in Court, although of course during the judges Appeal Hearings Desmond wore an ordinary business suit.

'Mrs Woods, it's so nice to meet you' he said, giving me a firm handshake. 'I'm looking forward to working with you on this interesting case you're bringing to Court'.

As I exchanged greetings with him, I couldn't help

noticing a distinct twinkle in his eye! The thought dawned on me that he seemed to be enjoying the prospect of the Hearing and the subsequent trial. I found the idea of being relaxed about the arguments to come pretty astonishing! But when the first of many Hearings commenced and I heard Desmond's presentation I began to understand how good he was at his job, and how having proper representation put things into a completely different gear. Here was a professional, who knew exactly what to do, and how to do it. And better still, he was working on our behalf! We promptly dubbed him God's man for the hour and left the Hearing much more confident than when we arrived. In many ways we were now redundant, and could let the professionals get on with things themselves.

But one of the ways in which we could still help our legal team was to act as research assistants. Scientology has a language all of its own, and most of the jargon it uses is pretty incomprehensible to those who have not come across it before. Even I, who had been immersed in the whole thing for eight years found the preparation of evidence so painstaking that I knew it was only by God's grace that I was able to complete what I was called upon to do.

I started to analyse every news article in which I had been quoted to see if I could substantiate what I had said with some sort of evidence of its truth. I found the work hard. I come from a long line of Ohio pioneers and I am by nature a person who likes starting things but soon tires of the day to day discipline necessary to build a strong line of defence.

Then I watched our team of professionals, going over things paragraph by paragraph, taking time over every small detail, which was so important if we were to stand a chance of winning. There were so many valuable things I began to learn from my highly trained and dedicated 'A' team! And to think that they were working so diligently and carefully just to ensure I had the right to tell things as I had discovered them to be.

Every single word of the leaflet called What The Scientologist's Don't Tell You which I had published in one of my early endeavours to inform people of what I considered to be the dangers of Scientology now had to be scrutinized for its accuracy. Hundreds of hours were also spent interviewing potential witnesses whose personal experiences would verify the claims I had made. I began to grasp afresh the importance of having the truth at the base of everything we say and do.

One interesting side effect of all this intense study and research was that I gained a new and deeper appreciation of the Bible. When I first became a Christian I found an incredible healing happening in my mind as I started reading it on a regular basis. I used to read it for four or five hours of the day, usually extremely early in the morning and even though I didn't have a deep theological understanding of what I read I was still left with an extraordinary sense of peace when I finished. Now again, several years later, in the throes of litigation with my head pounding after spending a day at the solicitors, I could pick up my Bible on the train on the way home and piece together my ragged thoughts. A verse of scripture in Romans 15:4 seems to back up what I was experiencing:

For whatsoever things were written a foretime were written for our learning, that we through patience and comfort of the Scriptures might have hope.

There was too much going on for me to totally understand all that was being done for me, and the way that it was affecting me and those who were working so hard on our behalf. It would be much later on that I would have the luxury of reflecting on what actually happened during that time.

But I wasn't fighting just for the right to tell our story but for the right for all Scientology members, past and present, to study any information they chose concerning Scientology and its founder. I wanted them to have the right to question the source of the material, its accuracy and any dissenting opinions that may exist on the truthfulness of its writings. So when I realised the extent to which I would be opposed on making this information available I became even more adamant that I should carry on speaking about it.

'Richard, I just sense there are many other people who have gone through trauma because of their involvement with Scientology who want to speak out about their experiences,' I said as we quickly put a meal together after another day in London. He nodded in agreement as I continued, 'and that's another reason why we need to keep on fighting through the legal system, to protect that right without the fear of having our character and reputations completely assassinated'.

'Bonnie, I always knew you were a fighter, but this is the biggest one we're ever got ourselves into', he said as he helped me take the plates out of the kitchen, 'But at least we're not on our own any more,' he said, giving me a wink.

It's hard to exaggerate the amount of work we needed to get through in order to bring all the facts before the court, which of course we needed to do in order to have a chance of winning the case. But, although we didn't know it, the Lord was working in the background, to make our task much easier than we could have ever imagined. The opportunity to publish the leaflet without fear of litigation was to come much sooner than we expected and in a way we couldn't have possibly thought of.

You will remember that because of my high level within the Scientology movement, I had had access to secret OT levels, which were forbidden by the movement to be seen by ordinary members of the public, or indeed Scientology members on a lower level. But I began to help the legal team prepare for a request for the judge to order Scientology to allow the court to see these hitherto secret writings, so that I could prove I had not libelled them when I had published the leaflet. It's interesting to note that although in Scientology thought the OT levels are considered to be highly dangerous to those who have not prepared for them by studying other writings by Hubbard, when it comes to it, they merely contain the more eccentric of his thoughts concerning pre-existence and stuff that reads as though it came straight from science fiction which of course he wrote extensively at one stage in his life. But, from their point of view it is material that they want to keep secret at any cost, and have gone to great lengths to keep this information from being widely available.

Alex very skilfully argued the point that these secret materials were necessary for all to see so that I could prove that I had not libelled their organisation but in fact had described them accurately and truthfully. She said again during the Hearing that it was necessary for this evidence to be disclosed as it went to the heart of the very case itself.

Both my Counsel and theirs were given prior knowledge of what the judge, Mr. Justice Popplewell would say the next day in court. Scientology's Counsel asked permission to show their client what the ruling would be, and the judge agreed, provided that our Counsel could do the same. But the next day when it became apparent that the judge would be ordering the circulation of a certain number of the secret levels, the team representing Scientology suddenly applied to discontinue their counterclaim. Before our eyes the lion's share of the case against us almost evaporated and Scientology was ordered to give us undertakings that we would not be sued for the publication of words similar to the leaflet we had distributed. It was a huge victory, and months later we were still coming to terms with the implications of being able to share that information with anyone who wished to see it.

It's difficult to explain how significant and unexpected this decision was. Just as Goliath fell when David released a well-aimed stone at the giant, who was so much more powerful than he, so suddenly our rich and powerful opponent was backing off and running for cover! It was surely as great a miracle as that incredible story from the Bible. We felt like celebrating, but we knew there were other battles ahead before we could claim the victory we sought.

We now began to look forward to the resolution of the libel action regarding Scientology's publication which had described me as an anti-religious hate campaigner and Escape as a front group for a deprogramming organisation which tried to force people away from their chosen faith through brainwashing. Their whole case against me was greatly reduced, now they had dropped their counterclaim against me. following their decision not to allow their secret OT level information to be made known. All they could bring to court was their right to speak out against my leaflet about them. It was as though doors were being shut in our favour as we walked down the narrow path which lead to victory.

To be fair, from time to time Scientology did make what I felt to be half-hearted attempts at negotiating a settlement, but in fact I always understood those attempts to be information-gathering sessions to try to find out whether I was weakening in my resolve. I never personally attended any of these meetings, but was represented by Tim and Sharon. Nevertheless, I had to decide fairly early on, what I would be prepared to accept in terms of settlement in case they wanted to pay me financial compensation before the case came to court. That was in fact a route I was always open to, remembering the biblical principle of settling with your adversary if he so agrees. But I guess the main bone of contention was always my request for a public apology in the High Court.

'I've prayed good and hard about the amount of money I would be prepared to accept from Scientology should they ever get to the point of offering to settle out of Court,' I said to Sharon one morning, as I pulled out papers from my briefcase, at the start of a new day of work .

'Oh, that's good, she said, smiling warmly. 'We've been having a chat about that too, in the office, and have come up with a figure that we feel might be appropriate, but not excessive'.

'Oh, great' I said, now curious to know what that figure might be , but still feeling happy about the figure I had in mind.

'You see, Alex, I'm fifty this year and as you know, in the Old Testament every fifty years was a jubilee year, when all debts were wiped out, and slaves were set free'. Alex nodded and said 'Yes, that's right – go on'.

'Well, the figure of £50,000 kept coming up in my mind each time Richard and I prayed about it , so I feel that's the one I should go for. I know it's not a lot for six years of litigation,' I added quickly, 'but it just feels right each time we pray' I concluded, looking at her carefully to try and gauge her reaction.

'Well, that's very interesting,' she said, with a twinkle in her eye. 'As I mentioned', she said, talking slowly and deliberately ' the team have been talking this one through as well, and we came up with a figure of.......£50,000' she said laughing, as she noted the look of delighted amazement on my face. 'Sounds like we all got it right eh?'

Meanwhile, while all the legal manoeuvrings were taking place, I still had a home and a family to look after. But Charlie, the minister of Trinity Methodist Church, where we were now attending, worked together with members of the church, and other Christian leaders in the town to make sure that we were well covered in prayer, and that our daily needs were provided.

'Bonnie – is that you? It's Charlie here, said the voice on the other end of the phone. 'Could you tell Richard that I've arranged to cover the costs of the repairs you need so that you can get your MOT renewed and for four new tyres as well. Hope that fits in with your plans OK. Sorry you weren't able to be at the prayer meeting last night – I know you got home late. But we were praying for you all'.

'Charlie, thank you so much. I really am grateful. I'll make sure Richard gets the message. I know he was getting a little worried about how long the car would last before it came to a full stop! See you Sunday, if not before.'

Our church family led by Charlie were just so supportive. When the car needed repairing, Charlie got it fixed. Did we need prayer support? Charlie would pray. Money running low? Charlie gave us grocery vouchers. Then, when he saw me looking particularly exhausted after one particularly hard week he arranged for me to be sent on a two week Christian retreat at Green Pastures, near Bournemouth.

Fortunately, all the visits to London were made during the time our two girls were at school, which meant their lives were not disrupted to any great extent. Sometimes of course the Hearings took longer than we had anticipated, making it impossible for us to be back home by the time they left school.

But help was at hand. Several mothers who also had children of a similar school age to ours used to invite them round for tea, so that we could pick them up later. Both Richard and I felt it was important to try to shield them from as much of the stress that we were experiencing as possible, and we pretty much succeeded in that, apart from the dreadful incident when we arrived home to discover a full scale demo going on outside our home!

Now a date for the trial had been set for June – the 4th to be precise. It was estimated that it would cover a period of nineteen days, and I wondered just how I would summon up the stamina that would be needed for such an ordeal.

Then I had a phone call from Tim which changed everything in a trice. Things had taken another turn – but this time for the good. In the best tradition of classic Westerns, the cavalry weren't just on the horizon, they were charging towards the covered wagons!

Chapter Twelve

In The Presence Of My Enemies – but Surrounded By My Friends

I'm convinced that somewhere in the universe there is a law that says that a telephone cannot ring unless the person for whom the call is intended for is either:

(a) in the bathroom,
(b) just starting a meal, which will go cold and become uneatable if left more than a few moments, or
(c) just on the point of falling asleep!

To be fair, on that memorable day in June when the call started to come through that would be life changing in its implications I hadn't been doing any of those things, but instead had had the phone almost glued to my ear for most of the afternoon as I tried to organise a rota of childminders for Chiara our two year old granddaughter for whom we had responsibility at that point in time. We were fortunate in having many kind friends who had volunteered to look after her whenever it was necessary, but in spite of their willing-ness, it still took time to organise all the details. And if that was all that needed to get ready for our marathon nineteen day trial it would have been more than sufficient to deal with, but it was in fact only one small part of all had to be done.

Getting to London for the best part of a month was going to be an expense for Richard and me, whatever mode of travel we chose, and in the end the train seemed to be the best option, given the state of our car, the horrendously early hour that we would have to leave if we were driving, as well as the problems of parking in London. But a month's train travel was beyond our meagre income. Although we were always busy giving advice and counselling to those who contacted us, we never felt it was right to charge for our services. Had we done so, we would have been quite wealthy – at this point we must have counselled well over 500 families. But in reality our monthly income was precarious to say the least, and didn't stretch to anything out of the ordinary or extra.

Then there was the problem of what to wear! It is just not acceptable to turn up at the High Court in London wearing the casual clothes we wore around the house each day! Richard only had one good suit, and he wasn't the right size to squeeze easily into other peoples' clothes. We seemed to have very few friends who, like Richard, were 6'2" tall with a 44" chest! I gained a reputation before the trial of approaching large men who came along to the church on a Sunday morning, with the same question

'Would it be possible for Richard to borrow the jacket you're wearing for a few days during the course of the next month?'

My own clothing needs were more easily met. I was fortunate in having several friends more or less my size, who didn't feel possessive about their clothes, for which I was so grateful.

On their own, none of the pre-trial problems we were having to sort out were huge, but collectively they seemed so, particularly against the backdrop of all the hassle we had experienced, together with six years of trying to deal with legal procedures and documents which were way out of our range. Add to all that the fact that I had not been sleeping well, so a ringing phone was not a sound I particularly wanted to hear.

But one by the one the problems were sorted. Several of our friends from alt.religion.scientology, a popular news-group for critics, had clubbed together to buy train tickets for the month, promises for the loan of clothes for Richard had started to come in and I'd just about organised a babysit-ting rota. All that now demanded my immediate attention was the phone, which was still making a noise in the hall like an impatient child who thinks it's been forgotten! I had to answer it, before it rung itself off the hook! Normally, I just let the answer phone machine pick up the calls, but on this occasion, just to stop the noise, I decided to take this call personally anyway.

By the time I made a dive for my noisy piece of tech-nology, it must have given out its tenth ring. I mechanically intoned my name, guessing that it was probably one of my friends wanting to alter their babysitting schedule for looking after Chiara – only to find myself talking to Tim the head of our legal team! I knew immediately that the phone call was an important one. Tim was a very busy person. He rarely rang, and then only when it would not have been appropriate for lesser members of his team to make the call.

'Bonnie? Hello, it's Tim here', he said in his clipped British accent, that somehow managed to have a warm, friendly edge to it. 'Have you a moment to talk? There has been a major development in your case which I wanted to discuss with you personally. I don't want to sound dramatic, but if you're not sitting down, you might like to.'

'Yes, yes of course,' I said, plonking myself down on the stairs, wondering what on earth he might have to say to me, adding, 'Please continue. I'm sitting down now.'

I bit my lip, trying to steel myself for whatever he might have to tell me. I just didn't know how I would cope if there were further complications to deal with in an already convoluted legal process. There seemed to have been so many twists and turns, and high and lows during the time we were preparing to go to trial, with first one and then another of the legal team leaving, to be replaced with a new person which meant we all had to get used to each other every time it happened.

The latest change had been just a month or two earlier when Sharon told us she had decided to resign from practising law, and therefore was going to step down from our case. Sad as we were to see her go, we were thrilled to welcome Ian on board, someone who we were to discover was thorough in the work he did, with a real eye for attention to detail. Was there to be another change in the legal team I wondered?

But the news Tim brought was better than I could have ever hoped. In fact he had to repeat it several times before it finally sunk in. Scientology was wanting to settle all legal action between us. They had totally capitulated. Not only that, but they were ready to meet all the settlement terms we had defined for them, including a public apology in the High Court on the morning the trial would have begun!

As Tim shared the news with me I sat there blinking back the tears, trying hard to concentrate on the further details that he had. Richard had now joined me, and was looking at me in a quizzical way, trying to guess what was being said to me. But before I could tell him the amazing news I needed to hear all that Tim had to say.

'.................so, in order to test whether their resolve was genuine, I stipulated that the personal damages you had requested be paid into your client account at Allen and Overy on Monday morning and then the apology can be given on Tuesday morning, the day the trial was due to begin. They agreed to that also, Bonnie, and as regards to personal damages, they put forward a figure of £55,000'.

£55,000! That was £5,000 more than I felt the Lord was wanting me to ask for. This was awesome!

'Tim, thank you so much. I don't quite know what to say. This is such good news. Richard's here, and we'll talk it through and get back to you.'

I put the phone down, and sat in stunned silence, trying to take in what I had just heard. Total capitulation. Public apology. £55,000! This was unprecedented – totally unheard of! And to think I almost didn't pick up the phone! Richard stood waiting patiently while I gathered my thoughts together, before trying to tell him everything in a complete rush.

'Hold on a minute Bonnie – hold on,' he said trying to keep up. 'One thing at a time! Let's just go through every point, bit by bit. Just tell me again, slowly this time, exactly what he actually said'.

I went through the conversation I had had with Tim, trying to remember as much detail as I could. The fact that I had to repeat what Tim had said to me made it sink in even more. We had won without a shot being fired. They had given in before a word had been said in Court. David had slain Goliath!

After Richard and I had gone over the details together we both felt that the next thing on our agenda was to ask the Lord what our next move should be. As we had many times before we sat down at the dining room table and gave God thanks for the news before asking Him to give us a peace about what we should do next. After praying for about half a hour we both felt settled about ringing Tim back, and instructing him to agree to their terms.

So, once again I found myself picking up the phone, but for reasons I would have never guessed just an hour before. I was soon talking again to Tim, who was waiting for our reaction to Scientology's proposal.

'Tim? Bonnie here. Just to let you know that Richard and I have prayed about everything that you told us, and we feel it's right to accept their apology and settlement terms. And please could you relay my appreciation of their offer of additional funds and say that God loves a cheerful giver! We're going to give the extra £5000 they offered to different Christian endeavours that could use our help.

Once I had finished speaking to Tim, we had some other phone calls to make. Too many in fact to contemplate. Tim had said that we could invite friends and prayer partners to hear the public apology read out in court, and we felt it was the least we could offer the people who had worked so hard on our behalf, and who had supported us so wonderfully. I gave one or two key people a call, and asked them to ring a few others. In no time at all the people we wanted to contact had been informed of this amazing turn of events.

And yet, as I started to think back over the last few months, maybe I shouldn't have been so surprised about the result after all. Richard and I attended church meetings where the gifts of the Holy Spirit operated. Great faith in God, and the things that He can do was generated at these meetings and remarkable things happened. Sometimes people were prayed for and were healed, on other occasions someone might receive a special word from God during the service. It might be a word of encouragement for someone going through a difficult time, or a word of warning or whatever. Thinking back to some of those meetings I remembered that on several occasions people had had a word from God for me, telling me that the battle was His and not mine, and that He would set a table for me in the presence of my enemies, just as God had promised originally to King David in probably his best known Psalm, Psalm 23. So maybe I shouldn't have been too surprised at the outcome after all. But I was. In fact, to use good old-fashioned British terminology, which I had now become more accustomed to, I was gob-smacked!

By the time Tuesday came round we were all in a joyous mood. The folks on the train from East Grinstead to London who were not part of our crowd must have wondered what was going on. But I couldn't really have bothered too much what people thought, it was just so wonderful to be celebrating after going through so many dark days. As I looked at the people surrounding us, I realised that God had made us very rich – not in monetary terms, but in the precious friends He had given us. God had spoken to me for years about how He was raising up 'Joshuas' and 'Calebs' for us – those who would understand and pray and support us through the difficult times – a people who didn't see giants in the promised land but who saw difficulties as little grass hoppers in the face of a Sovereign God's protection and deliverance. Now here they all were, on a train journey packed full of laughter and love.

Ron was there of course, smiling broadly, and making sure everyone was OK. And another dear friend, Caroline, had offered to come and look after Chiara during the hearing, and again afterwards at the champagne reception that Allen and Overy had arranged. I appreciated Caroline, a mother of five so much, the love of Jesus just shone from her. But she is also a very practical lady, and in a very gentle, humble sort of way was always alongside when help was needed. Then there was our friend Mary who had travelled from Ireland. When we first met her she had recently left the Scientology organisation, and we had been able to do some counselling work with her. A pretty woman, with a lovely singing voice, she too was involved in litigation with Scientology for a number of years, and was herself suing Scientology among other things for the violation of her constitutional rights. To our delight she had recommitted her life to the Lord shortly after her visit to us and had made huge strides in her Christian walk since. Sadly Charlie wasn't with us on the train, but assured us that he would meet us at the High Court.

News travels fast, and the media had got wind of what was going to take place that morning. As we got out of our taxi which had brought us to the High Court from Allen and Overy's offices we were surrounded by a bevy of press photographers and television crews, all wanting a picture or a quote from me that they could use in their papers or in their next TV bulletin. This was unlike the press interviews I had done before. Everyone pressing for a statement at once was quite a new experience.

Ian, our recently acquired solicitor, looking businesslike but relaxed, stepped into the breach and told them all that I wouldn't be making any comments until after the hearing was finished, when I would be happy – not the word I would have chosen, but I knew what he meant – to answer their questions.

Leaving the noise and bustle of the press and the London traffic behind us we stepped into the rarefied atmosphere of the High Court building itself. The first people I spotted were Beverley and Sharon, waiting patiently outside the courtroom for us. I was so thrilled to see them, and to be able to thank them personally for all that they had done for us.

Our next act was to file into the courtroom to hear the statement read. The gallery was packed with well wishers and members of the press. Michael, our Q.C. was there, ready to read out the statement of the history of the case. After Scientology made the decision to withdraw their counter-claim they replaced their entire legal team led by Hodge Malek, and procured the services of Mr. Moloney, Q.C., who was there with his solicitor Peter Hodkin.

After Michael had read out our statement Mr. Moloney proceeded to read their apology. Those wanting to read the full text of both statements can access them on the world-wide web_ Afterwards I resisted the urge to give Michael a big hug and settled for squeezing his arm. The whole thing, which had taken a good six years of our life, was over in just six minutes – one for every year of the case! I felt as though I was in some kind of daze, which left me confused as to what was actually said by whom. Later on I needed to look at Stephen's UK Critics web page to refresh my memory as to what actually was said and done!

We left the court and met some of the press who were crowded outside the door and I made the first statement there and answered their questions. There was also a crowd of photographers and TV journalists waiting for us on the famous front steps, wanting to get something for their bulletins later that day.

Several times over the six years we had struggled with the case it had seemed that nothing was going right. But on this wonderful day, everything seemed to be going our way. Even the British weather was kind to us! The sun shone brightly as we left the High Court building.

I was particularly pleased that the sun was shining that day. One of the reasons was that on the train my friend from Ireland, Mary, had presented me with a gift. It was a diamante brooch spelling simply the name of Jesus. I had pinned it on my lapel, and as the sun shone onto the stones, it sparkled, causing everyone to notice it, so much so that it was mentioned in several of the press articles the following morning. Before trying to answer the many questions that the press wanted to put to me I was keen to read the statement I had prepared the day before:

Sometimes when it was hard to carry on, especially when my husband and I were litigating in person, I got so discouraged that I didn't think I could go on. Not even one more hearing. A friend of mine had programmed my computer so that a picture of Lisa McPherson pops up on the screen each time I turned it on. For those of you who have not heard of Lisa she was a long term member of Scientology who died after a 17 day stay at the Scientology headquarters, the Fort Harrison Hotel in Clearwater, Florida. Her name and memory burns bright in my mind these days as does the names of Noah Lottick, Patrick Vic, and Richard Collins and others who may be nameless to us but are more than precious memories to their families and friends. I continued to stand because I couldn't bear the thought that their families mourned their loss in vain. I needed to speak the truth about Scientology as I understood it to be.

I believed that it needed to be proclaimed so that captives could be set free-the prisoners released and the broken-hearted could become whole again. I am not ashamed of my Christian commitment to their plight.

Then questions started to be fired at me from all sides. Of course, I tried to answer everything as honestly as I could, wanting also to speak as much about our faith in God as I could. What I didn't know was that unlike other times that I had been interviewed by the press, when they didn't want to know about my Christian faith, this time some had been instructed by their editors to focus on the 'Jesus thing' – which was just fine by me!

One of the reporters asked me how it had been for us during the heart of the harassment. I replied that it had been a 'Job' experience. He looked puzzled. 'What kind of experience is that?' he replied. Charlie stepped in, and quickly explained about the Old Testament character who went through many trials before God finally vindicated him. 'I think I need to read about that man,' was the reporter's pithy reply!

The Scientologists also handed out a statement to the press, which was a toned down version of what they had said in court, making it sound as though they had dropped the case against us because they felt sorry for us, and the fact that we wouldn't be able to pay costs if they had won the case. The facts are that huge amounts of money had been expended in preparing this court case – some people estimate that Scientology spent almost two million pounds on the case! But one of the most positive things to result from the settlement was that Scientology accepted an undertaking which prevented them from repeating the libels against me. So, if they tried to mount another hate campaign against me, they would face prison and contempt charges.

After answering as many questions as I could, we trooped off with our friends to the pub across the road from the High Court for a champagne reception. God had turned around everything in a trice. And now, instead of having to face nineteen days of interrogation, Richard and I started to look forward to a fortnight away at a farm in Devon, with our little granddaughter for a much needed rest and 'catch-up' time!

We were of course interested to find out the next day how our story had been covered by the newspapers, and we were pleased to see that the reporting had been fair and well balanced. And we found the press interest into our story to be huge. For the next three or four weeks the phone never seemed to stop ringing. We had always had a policy of praying about which radio, TV or press interviews to accept, and on occasions felt it right to turn down some pretty high profile ones. Now our policy would really be of value, and our need to make right choices went into overdrive.

But our battles were not over! We still had Escape, our counselling ministry which was increasingly busy as people got to know that there was somewhere they could go where people were prepared to listen to what they, or their loved ones had gone through, and to learn that there is always light at the end of the tunnel – and that Light is the One that God sent to earth, 2000 years ago, Jesus, The Light of the World.

Our strategy for the future is simple and clear – to stand and peacefully oppose. It seems to be summed up in a scripture found in the New Testament.

"And let us not grow weary while doing good, for in due season we shall reap if we do not lose heart [Gal 6:9]

This for us, forms the way forward. It would be easy to step down now that we have achieved our own personal victory, but the Lord has opened a door for us to walk through, a door that will never be closed, which is a door to freedom. We know that love never fails. So we stand in peace and love to oppose that which has proved to us to be a danger to the liberty and freedom of those who became ensnared with it. We invite all those who have loved ones involved with Scientology to come and stand with us. We want, with God's grace and mercy, to help those voiceless ones to have a voice that will be heard. And then, having done all, to stand.

Appendix

The following is a factual account of the roots of Scientology and an overview of its basic teaching. It contains some material that the Scientologists have previously tried to suppress, but which I am able to publish here to re-enforce the statements made in my leaflet What the Scientologists Don't Tell You Many of the years we spent in litigation with Scientology were taken up preparing a defence to the counterclaim they had brought against us in response to my libel action. When it became apparent during a very important hearing, that the judge would be ordering the discovery into evidence of a certain number of the secret Operating Thetan levels, the team representing Scientology suddenly applied to discontinue their counterclaim. As a term of the discontinuance, Scientology was required to sign undertakings agreeing that I could not be sued for the information or similar words contained in the leaflets I had published.

So for the first time I am able to publish information which I gathered over the last nine years while researching documents concerning the life and writings of L.Ron Hubbard and the teachings of Scientology and Dianetics. I gratefully acknowledge that the finest and most reliable material I studied was the published works of Jon Atack. Particularly valuable was his book A Piece of Blue Sky .I also consulted the booklet The Total Freedom Trap and many of his published research papers.

WHAT THE SCIENTOLOGISTS DON'T TELL YOU

Dianetics and Scientology were created by adventure and science fiction writer L.Ron Hubbard. Shortly before publishing his first textbook in 1950, Hubbard told several people that the best way to become rich was to start a religion. Hubbard's wealth when he died in 1986 amounted to almost $650 million, all of it derived from the Church of Scientology.

Hubbard made numerous false claims about his life. In fact, he was neither a nuclear physicist, an explorer, nor a war hero. His claims to have studied with mystics in China, Tibet and India are entirely false. He was asked to leave a civil engineering degree course for deficiency of scholarship.

Born in the USA in 1911, Ron Hubbard grew up in the northern state of Montana. His father, Harry, failed at a variety of careers before joining the Navy when his son was six. From then until he was twelve Ron was largely in the care of his mother and her sisters in a household dominated by grandfather Lafayette Waterbury. His grandfather was a veterinary surgeon who for a while owned a horse ranch, but Hubbard would later claim that Lafe Waterbury's holdings amounted to 'a quarter of Montana.' This pattern of exaggeration would be Hubbard's way over and over again. The creator of Scientology inflated his life to epic proportions.

Many other outlandish claims were made by Hubbard about his childhood. He broke broncos at the age of three and became a blood brother of the Blackfoot Indians at four. The truth is more prosaic – Hubbard was scared of horses, and elsewhere admitted that his information about the Blackfoot was second hand. This didn't stop a zealous eighth-blood called Tree Many Feathers, who also happened to be a Scientologist, from retroactively making Hubbard a blood brother to make true the lie.

Hubbard's interest in the human mind was allegedly sparked when he was twelve, and met eccentric Navy Commander 'Snake' Thompson while aboard ship traversing the Panama Canal. Nothing in Hubbard's extensive teenage journals reflects any enquiry into the Freudian mysteries, however. A few weeks spent in the Orient in his mid-teens was blown up into a five year study with gurus in China, India and Tibet. Factually, Hubbard did not visit either India or Tibet, and the diaries of his journeys made no reference to the wisdom of the East beyond the comment that the monks sounded 'like bullfrogs'. He summed up his holiday by saying 'the trouble with China is, there are too many Chinks here,' and suggested that the Great Wall be turned into a 'roller coaster.'

Hubbard's later claims to be a nuclear physicist were based on a failing grade in a short course in Atomic and Molecular Physics. He was placed on probation and then dropped out of George Washington University where he was ostensibly studying Civil Engineering. During a Summer vacation, Hubbard led the first of his purported 'expeditions' – a student trip aboard a schooner to the Caribbean to re-enact various pirate battles. Hubbard wrote bitterly of the failure of this expedition at the time, but later made claims that it had provided the Hydrographic Office and the University of Michigan with 'invaluable data for the furtherance of their research.' There is no record of this invaluable data at either institution.

Probably to avoid the lawsuits threatened by disgruntled fellow students from the Caribbean Motion Picture Expedition, Hubbard fled to Puerto Rico. Typically, a brief spell as assistant to a mineralogist searching for manganese would later be recast by Hubbard as his own direction of 'the first complete mineralogical survey of Puerto Rico.'

During the 1930's, Hubbard struggled to establish himself as a writer. His articles and stories included Navy Pets and Man-Killers of the Air. He gained a reputation for his ability to produce reams of adventure stories for the pulp fiction market. In 1933, Hubbard entered into the first of three marriages. His son 'Nibs' was born in 1934, followed by a daughter, Catherine, in 1936. Despite his huge output, penny –a—word fees could not support both his extravagant lifestyle and his family. His wife, Polly, had to rely on the generosity of Hubbard's parents.

Somehow Hubbard talked himself into the Explorers' Club of New York, and managed to outfit a small boat by proposing an expedition to Alaska. His wife Polly joined him. The expedition consisted largely of weeks stranded in harbour writing sniping letters to the providers of his failed equipment, appearing on Ketchikan radio and promoting himself through the pages of the Seattle Star.

By the time he returned from Ketchikan, Hubbard had decided to abandon his precarious career as a pulp fiction writer and follow in his father's footsteps. Hubbard joined the US Navy Reserve five months before the Japanese attack on Pearl Harbour. When the US entered the war, Hubbard was sent to Australia. He was posted as an 'intelligence officer', which inevitably led to his claims to have been in US Navy Intelligence. In fact, his job was to report sightings of ships and planes, and to censor mail.

Hubbard's posting lasted a few months. Ordering him back home, the US Naval Attache to Australia wrote 'By assuming unauthorized authority and attempting to perform duties for which he has no qualifications, he became the source of much trouble .. This officer is not satisfactory for independent duty assignment. He is garrulous and tries to give impressions of his importance. He also seems to think that he has unusual ability in most lines. These characteristics indicate that he will require close supervision for satisfactory performance of any intelligence duty.' Hubbard's own account of his return home differed markedly. He said he had been the 'first US returned casualty from the Far East.'

In New York, Hubbard was briefly subjected to the recommended close supervision, but in the chaos of war it was relatively easy for a man of Hubbard's silver tongue to side step the advice of his superior. Hubbard captained the refit of a small vessel in Boston harbour. Contrary to claims made in the cult's literature, the YPP-422 did not serve 'with British and American anti-submarine warfare vessels in the North Atlantic;' least, not while Hubbard was aboard.

In spite of the opinion of the Commander of the Boston Navy Yard that Hubbard was 'not temperamentally fitted for independent command,' Hubbard was transferred to oversee the fitting of an anti-submarine boat in Portland, Oregon. It was in the PC 815 that the self-proclaimed war hero saw his only battle. Twelve miles off the Oregon coast, while on its first or shakedown cruise, the PC 815 reported submarine activity. Hubbard drew every available vessel and airship into the fray and fought a 55-hour contest with what was later identified as a 'magnetic deposit'. Hubbard claimed to have damaged not one but two Japanese submarines. There is no evidence to support this claim. Before the PC 815 docked, and he was removed from his last command, Hubbard fired on the Los Coronados islands, which although luckily uninhabited were nonetheless Mexican territory.

So began the final chapter of Hubbard's war time service. Two years before hostilities ended, Hubbard reported to hospital with an ulcer. Reviewing Hubbard's battle, Rear Admiral Braisted wrote 'Consider this officer lacking in the essential qualities of judgment, leadership and cooperation. He acts without forethought as to probable results. He is believed to have been sincere in his efforts to make his ship efficient and ready. Not considered qualified for command or promotion at this time. Recommend duty on a large vessel where he can be properly supervised.' This time the advice was followed and, after three months on the sick list for an ulcer that was never detected by X-ray, Hubbard was posted to the USS Algol. The Algol was readied for service during the next months. Shortly before she set sail for her first taste of combat, Hubbard was posted to a course in military government on the campus of Princeton University. Of course, he would later falsely claim to be a graduate of that august academy.

It is probable that Hubbard was being trained for the occupation of Japan, a frightening prospect in the face of Japan's total resistance. Instead, Hubbard spent the last months of the war in hospital, once more complaining of an ulcer. While in hospital his eyesight deteriorated (at least according to his own performance on eye charts at the time). This would lead to the claim that he was 'crippled and blinded' at the end of World War II, as a consequence of his wounds. Hubbard would later speak of an addiction to barbiturate drugs that probably began as a treatment for his ulcer.[1]

Hubbard would make enormous boasts about his position and prowess as a war hero. It was all puffery. He never actually saw combat.

Hubbard was deeply involved with the practice of

Aleister Crowley's 'Sex Magick.' In 1946, he participated in rituals aimed at reincarnating the goddess Babylon, the antichristian force of the book of Revelation. Shortly thereafter, he wrote in one of his journals 'All men are my slaves'.

Rather than returning to his family with his discharge from hospital, Hubbard headed to Pasadena, where he took up with the notorious scientist and 'sex magician,' Jack Parsons. Parsons was a founder of Jet Propulsion Laboratories and the inventor of solid rocket fuel. A crater on the moon is named after him. Appropriately, it is on the so called dark side. Parsons had long been consumed by the writings of Aleister Crowley, the self-styled 'Beast 666'. Crowley was a voluble critic of Christianity who spent a lifetime assembling magical rituals in preparation for his pivotal role in the overthrow of Christendom. He died in 1947 a broken drug addict.

Hubbard's tall stories either fascinated or appalled Parsons' guests and lodgers. Within days of his arrival, he had seduced Parsons' girlfriend, Sara Northrup. Determined to climb above his damaged feelings, Parsons enlisted Hubbard as a 'magical partner' and they began a series of rituals and invocations supposed to incarnate the Whore of Babylon spoken of in St John's Revelation. Crowley called his teachings 'Sex Magick' and it is clear that his rituals included homosexual activity. Hubbard would later insist that all gays were backstabbers. But it is very possible that Parsons and Hubbard undertook homosexual rituals in their attempt to attract a woman capable of gestating the Whore of Babylon. Hubbard felt no shame at his involvement with Sex Magick, and although they never actually met, Hubbard would later boast that Crowley was his 'very good friend'.[2]

In March 1946, Marjorie Cameron turned up at Parsons'

house, and willingly joined in the rituals. Soon afterwards, Hubbard took Parsons' savings to Florida saying he would buy yachts there and sell them in California at a profit. The whole affair ended with a furious Parsons filing suit and the dissolution of the partnership. Parsons was left high and dry. Hubbard married Sara Northrup, without first divorcing his first wife.

After the war, Hubbard languished. His claim for a disability pension was denied by the US Navy, but eventually accepted by the Veterans Administration. He would receive a small pension for the rest of his days, despite claims to have cured himself completely by 1950 with his revolutionary new science, Dianetics.

Using what he had learned from Crowley's books and popular texts on Freudian therapy and hypnosis, Hubbard fashioned a 'science of the mind'. To the horror of Scientology leaders, many of Hubbard's private papers came into public view in a spectacular court case in 1984. Among these papers were various magical rituals, and handwritten self-hypnotic affirmations including 'Men are my slaves.' This calls into question the true emphasis of his 'science of mind.' After a sojourn in Georgia with his mentor Arthur J. Burks, who believed that the world is populated with tiny invisible entities, Hubbard wrote to his agent that he had a book with more selling angles than anything he had ever seen. At around the same time, a shortage of funds led to an embarrassing conviction for cheque fraud.

In August 1947, Astounding Science Fiction published Hubbard's story The End is Not Yet. In the story a nuclear physicist ends a dictatorship with the invention of a new philosophy. Hubbard set about recreating himself in this new image. He began to tell friends that the best way to make a million was to start a religion. Hubbard took ideas abandoned by Freud,[3] mixed in a little Crowley and his own considerable knowledge of hypnosis, and came up with Dianetics.

Before settling on the libido theory, Freud had utilised a hypnotic method whereby his patients were asked to focus on traumatic incidents. By recounting these painful memories, patients would discover earlier memories of a similar type. By finding and recounting the earliest memory on what both Freud and Hubbard called a 'chain', the patient would be released from its subconscious influence. Freud had abandoned the method because its positive effects did not endure. Such methods also tended to promote and increase dependency upon the therapist. Hubbard created an elaborate new terminology, and added a few hypnotic tricks of his own.[4] Dianetics was born.

Dianetics did not burst upon the world through the pages of a learned journal. Rather it was announced in Astounding Science Fiction by editor John Campbell as a 'new science.' Campbell raved 'Its power is almost unbelievable; it proves the mind not only can but does rule the body completely; following the sharply defined basic laws Dianetics sets forth, physical ills such as ulcers, asthma and arthritis can be cured, as can all other psychosomatic ills.'

A Foundation had been established in anticipation, but the rush must have astonished even Hubbard. Before the publisher withdrew Dianetics: The Modern Science of Mental Health, the book had scaled the bestseller lists, with the sale of 150,000 copies.

By elimination of the most fundamental subliminal trauma, or basic-basic, Dianetic processing would lead to complete rationality, the state of Clear. According to Dianetics: The Modern Science of Mental Health a Clear would have no compulsions, repressions, or psychosomatic ills. He would have full control of his imagination, and a near perfect memory. During the course of processing, IQ would 'soar' by as much as '50 points,' and the Clear would be 'phenomenally intelligent.'

Dianetics would rescue broken marriages. Through its practice the individual would be freed of psychoses and neuroses. Among the 'psychosomatic' conditions Dianetics claimed to cure were asthma, poor eyesight, colour blindness, hearing deficiencies, stuttering, allergies, sinusitis, arthritis, high blood pressure, coronary trouble, dermatitis, ulcers, migraine, conjunctivitis, morning sickness, alcoholism and the common cold. Even tuberculosis would be alleviated. Dianetics would also have 'a marked effect upon the extension of life.' A Clear could do a computation which a normal person 'would do in half an hour, in ten or fifteen seconds.'

Hubbard said he had examined and treated 273 people and found the 'single and sole source of aberration.' It was insisted that Dianetics was effective on anyone, who had not had 'a large portion of his brain removed,' or been 'born with a grossly malformed nervous structure.' And Dianetics could be practised straight from the book without further training. The process would take between 30 and 1,200 hours, and with its completion the person would be Clear, and so entirely free of irrationality and every psychosomatic ailment. The cult has never seen fit to revoke any of these outrageous claims and continues to publish and sell the book, without revision or apology.

Dianetics Foundations sprouted in the major cities of America. The psychotherapy community gave signs of either alarm or support. Fritz Perls, the father of Gestalt Therapy, lauded Dianetics. Rollo May, father of Existential Therapy, lambasted it. The American Psychological Association circulated a cautious warning: 'While suspending judgement concerning the eventual validity of the claims made by the author of Dianetics, the association calls attention to the fact that these claims are not supported by the empirical evidence of the sort required for the establishment of scientific generalizations. In the public interest, the association, in the absence of such evidence, recommends to its members that the use of the techniques peculiar to Dianetics be limited to scientific investigations to test the validity of its claims.'

Hubbard had already started his lifelong war against the psychological and psychiatric professions. Apart from a small, bizarre and unsuccessful study in the Los Angeles Dianetic Foundation, Hubbard's new science would never be subjected to scientific scrutiny by his followers. Instead euphoric testimonials are presented as 'proof' of the efficacy of Hubbard's techniques.

After a few months the Dianetic bubble burst. The book's publisher and the medical doctor who had written the book's effusive foreword both resigned from the Board of the Hubbard Dianetic Research Foundation. The overblown claims had proved untrue. Dr Joseph Winter was particularly concerned by Hubbard's advocacy of amphetamine drugs or *speed*.[5] The hammer blow came when Sara filed for divorce. Hubbard's response was immediate. He kidnapped their eleven-month-old daughter and fled to Cuba. The American Medical Association was about to initiate a lawsuit for practising medicine without a licence. The time had come to flee the country.

From Cuba, Hubbard denounced Sara, and even several of his loyal associates, to the FBI as 'communists.' Had it not been for Kansas oil millionaire Don Purcell, this might have been the end for Dianetics. Purcell flew Hubbard back to the US, and a meeting with Sara was arranged. After three months without her daughter, a distraught Sara was persuaded to accept a quiet divorce, and sign a bizarre document in which she said that Hubbard was 'a fine and brilliant man.' Privately, Sara would later write that Hubbard was as 'mad as a hatter. His sickness is not just destructive it is also contagious. I hate to think how many weak people have been harmed by this man.' For his part, Hubbard would claim that they were never married, and that their daughter Alexis, to whom he originally dedicated his book Science of Survival, was Parsons' child.

Hubbard fell out with Purcell within a year, moving to Phoenix, Arizona. In his attempts to save Dianetics, Purcell had bought the original Dianetic Foundation from bankruptcy and along with it apparently acquired the rights to the name and the subject too. Hubbard had to come up with something new – and quickly. The penny-a-word pulp fiction writer, famous for his output, created Scientology from whole cloth in a matter of weeks.

If Dianetics had been a science of mind, then Scientology would be a science of spirit. Incorporating many of Aleister Crowley's ideas[6] – even appropriating the cross of Crowley's Ordo Templi Orientis – Scientology would soon be characterised by its creator as a religion. In this way there would be nothing to fear from charges of practising medicine without a licence, and ultimately tax exemption could be achieved.

Hubbard incorporated the 'Church' of Scientology secretly in 1953, following a letter to an associate in which he asked her opinion of the 'religion angle.' Scientology probably became a 'religion' in the USA to avoid further investigation by the American Medical Association into Hubbard's many far-fetched claims. These included the ridiculous claim that Scientology would even cure cancer.

In December 1953, Hubbard secretly incorporated three churches, in Camden, New Jersey – the Church of American Science, the Church of Spiritual Engineering and the Church of Scientology. Tithes were to be paid by the other churches to the Church of American Science, which was represented as a Christian Church. Perversely, Hubbard later explained that this Church could be used to recruit Christians so that they could be moved on to something 'better,' such as the Church of Scientology.[7] Hubbard wrote to a deputy extolling the financial benefits of adopting the 'religion angle.'

Scientology's numerous claims to be compatible with Christian belief cannot be taken seriously. For example, in Hubbard's view, we are all Thetans, spirits who participated in the creation of the universe, and have reincarnated since the beginning of time. With the invention of Scientology came new counselling procedures, including the bizarre instruction to make mental images of God and to 'waste, accept under duress, desire and finally be able to take or leave alone' these images or ideas.[8]

In the notes of a limited South African edition of his Phoenix Lectures, we find the statement that God is 'the greatest problem producer' and further 'God just happens to be the trick of this universe.' Hubbard believed that this is just one of many universes. The others apparently do not suffer from the 'problem' of God.

Alongside the new Churches came the Freudian Foundation of America. Hubbard teamed up with a diploma mill – Sequoia University – and began to issue degrees ranging from Bachelor to Doctor of Scientology, as well as Freudian Psycho-analyst and Doctor of Divinity. Such diplomas continued to be issued until Sequoia University was closed down by the California Department of Education in 1958. Hubbard's own doctorate in philosophy also came from Sequoia.

Hubbard ventured into his own past lives publishing an account of his supposed memories in Scientology – A History of Man. Here, Hubbard scoffed at evolutionary theorists, insisting that humanity is descended from clams. In lectures recorded in the early 1950s, Hubbard declaimed about the inhabitants of Mars and Venus, and spoke of interplanetary civilizations to which we had allegedly all belonged. This nonsense was all put forward as hard, scientific fact and none of it has been withdrawn from current editions.

In the 1950s, in his peculiar and rambling bulletin The Scientologist: a Manual of the Dissemination of Material, Hubbard recommended legal action against anyone who used his techniques without permission (he called such defectors squirrels): 'The purpose of the suit is to harass and discourage rather than to win. The law can be used very easily to harass, and enough harassment on somebody who is simply on the thin edge anyway, well knowing that he is not authorized, will generally be sufficient to cause his professional decease. If possible, of course, ruin him utterly.'

Hubbard also ordered the use of private detectives against such defectors. This policy was to grow to epic proportions in the ensuing decades, spreading across continents and successfully silencing most of the cult's critics.

Don Purcell eventually abandoned any claim to Dianetics and relinquished all title to the term and its texts to Hubbard. Dianetics and Scientology were united under Hubbard's control.

Scientologists undertake hundreds of hours of 'counselling,' paying as much as £500 per hour. The counselling actually heightens suggestibility, and undermines the critical faculties. Indeed, in a 1955 letter, Hubbard offered his 'brainwashing' techniques to the FBI. While being promised that through Scientology individuals will regain their 'self-determinism,' Scientology actually leads to unquestioning acceptance of Hubbard's belief system and the erosion of independent thought. To complete the elaborate and lengthy steps of Hubbard's 'Bridge to Total Freedom' takes years and costs in the region of £200,000. Some Scientologists have lost their homes and businesses to pay for increasingly expensive courses.

By the mid-1950s, Scientology was a franchised 'Church' with outposts in every English -speaking country. Privately, Hubbard wrote to the FBI offering to sell them his 'brainwashing' techniques. He boasted 'we can brainwash faster than the Russians – twenty seconds to total amnesia.' He was urging his followers to go into hospitals and offer cures to polio victims. He even claimed that Scientology would cure cancer.

After the original Dianetic boom, Hubbard's following was small, but the revenues were still sufficient for him to buy a Georgian manor house in Sussex, moving there with third wife Mary Sue Whipp and their children in 1959.

Even before the dissolution of the early Dianetic Foundations, Hubbard had adopted the use of a refined lie detector to help in tracking down traumatic memories. Soon the inventor of this machine – Volney Mathieson – was all but forgotten and it became the Hubbard Electropsychometer, or E-meter. With the defection of Hubbard's eldest son, Nibs, the E-meter was used to root out confessions of hidden desires to harm Scientology or Hubbard. Questionnaires with hundreds of invasive questions were printed, and

Hubbard's followers were interrogated while attached to the E-meter. Scientologists were expected to reveal every last detail of their lives, including their sexual practices and anything else for which they might be blackmailed. All responses were written down, and, where any harm to Scientology or its creator was intimated, or anything illegal or potentially embarrassing was admitted, these reports were placed in the offender's Ethics file. At first such interrogations were simply styled Security Checks. Later this would be softened to Confessionals and ultimately Integrity Processing. The same lists are still in use whatever the euphemism. Few people are willing to stand up against an organisation that has written details of their every moral transgression. More people have left Scientology than are now members, but very few of these tens of thousands will risk their reputations to speak publicly of the treatment they received while in the cult.

Most often, recruitment into Scientology begins with a personality test. The 'Oxford Capacity Analysis' was written by a former merchant seamen unschooled in psychology. The 200-question test has no connection with Oxford University, and demands extensive personal information. The Scientologists have a history of using material supposedly received in confidence to harass former members. New recruits were callously termed raw meat by Hubbard.

By the early 1960s, a complicated series of steps had grown into what Hubbard styled The Bridge. Hubbard had retreated from his original claims – though none of them would be withdrawn from Dianetics: The Modern Science of Mental Health – it now took tens of hundreds procedures to achieve the state of Clear. And Hubbard was investigating states beyond the complete rationality promised at Clear. He now offered a god-like state that he called Operating Thetan. With the application of his techniques, his followers would be able to leave their bodies voluntarily and travel to any part of the universe. Their wishes, or postulates, would come true, leading to complete material success. In his own deranged mind, Ron Hubbard had become a god maker.

In May 1963, Hubbard issued a bulletin entitled Routine 3, Heaven in which he claimed to have visited heaven on two occasions. He asserted that at some time everybody else had also been to heaven. Despite public claims of Scientology's compatibility with Christianity, here Hubbard spoke of his prolonged refusal to believe in 'a Christian heaven, God and Christ.' His first visit was some 43 million, million years ago. Heaven was in fact a place where spirits were hypnotically implanted in between lives. Hubbard insisted 'Heaven is a false dream and ... the old religion was based on a very painful lie, a cynical betrayal.' He signed off saying 'when we finally manage to communicate with beetles under rocks and free them, we'll no doubt find the Creator of Heaven who 43 + Trillion years ago designed and built the Pearly Gates and entrapped us all.' Of his own teachings, Hubbard would say, 'New Religions always overthrow the false Gods of the old.'

During the 1960s, Scientology received much attention from the media and from governments. Several Australian states briefly tried to ban the practice of Scientology, leading to the establishment of the Church of the New Faith. A British government Enquiry was highly critical of the cult's teachings and practices, the most scandalous being the Fair Game doctrine, whereby critics of the cult could be 'tricked, sued or lied to or destroyed [punctuation sic].' The other heinous practice introduced by Hubbard at this time was disconnection whereby Scientologists are forbidden to speak to anyone critical of the cult. This has had the frequent effect of splitting up families. The media attention these practices sparked had an unfortunate side effect: the cult was publicised and attracted a much larger following. Scientology began to expand beyond the English-speaking world into Europe.

In a secret internal directive, Hubbard explained, 'We are responsible for getting people through to Clear and OT and reserve therefore as our right the use of any means or force necessary to accomplish this.' To his intelligence department, he explained the objectives of his religion forcefully. Scientology's targets were: 'Depopularizing the enemy to a point of total obliteration. Taking over control or allegiance of the heads or proprietors of all news media. Taking over the control or allegiance of key political figures.'

A new and firm 'governing policy' was laid out for cult staff: 'Make money, make more money, make others produce so as to make even more money.'

With the secret 'Upper Levels,' Scientologists seek to achieve supernatural powers. Several thousand former Scientologists who have taken these courses can attest that the techniques are completely ineffective, leading only to a progressive dissociation from reality.

A belief in reincarnation is required in Scientology. In the third secret Upper Level, Hubbard asserted that 75 million years ago, the galactic ruler, Xenu, rounded up the populations of 76 planets and had them brought to earth. Here their bodies were dumped near volcanoes which were blown up with hydrogen bombs. The individual spirits (or 'thetans') were collected and 'implanted' with 36 days of movies depicting the symbols of Christianity and all the social, religious and technological phenomena which have since ensued. These spirits were then gathered into 'clusters,' and everyone currently alive is supposedly a mass of such clustered spirits.

In this way, Hubbard exploited the traditional belief in demon possession, and induced multiple personality disorders in his followers. It is not surprising that a number of Scientologists have either committed suicide or ended up in psychiatric hospitals.

Hubbard had left England in 1966 and after a spell in North Africa moved to the Spanish Canary Islands, where he was putting the finishing touches to his third Operating Thetan level. Hubbard was to assert that anyone finding out about this material would die within days. That is, anyone who had not paid for and received the many tortuous Dianetic and Scientology levels leading up to Operating Thetan level three.

Scientologists are assured that they have reincarnated over thousands of millions of millions of years. Hubbard used the term quadrillion. His followers were taught that they have lived through many interplanetary civilizations. Before the beginning of time, spirits or Thetans existed, separate from one another (Thetans were not created, but have existed for all time and actually precede the creation of time). With the creation of energy and matter, Thetans have gradually become solidified into matter. The usual method of entrapment has been through "implanting," where the Thetan is hypnotised and given positive suggestions which limit its powers. This process, according to Hubbard, has been going on in this universe for four quadrillion Years (4,000,000,000,000,000, rather than the mere 8-20,000,000 of contemporary scientific belief). However, our universe is just one in a series.

Scientology seeks to return the Thetan's power by stripping away implants and using drills to heighten extrasensory perception and ability. The goal of these procedures is an Operating Thetan or OT – a being who can act independently of his physical body, and can cause physical events to occur through sheer force of will. The Operating Thetan will supposedly be capable of dismissing illness and psychological disorder in others at will.

The Scientologist generally undertakes hundreds of hours of preparation prior to taking the first section of the Operating Thetan level courses – OT 1. OT 2 consists of over a hundred pages of handwritten lists of opposites, such as "create – create no". These are supposedly the basic positive suggestions from implants administered 75 million years ago. These implants were part of the so-called OT 3 incident.

According to Hubbard, 75 trillion years ago there was a confederation of 76 planets, including Earth. The Galactic Confederation – the title comes from the science fiction of E.E. 'Doc' Smith – was ruled by Xenu. Overpopulation was a serious problem, which Xenu resolved by murdering many of the inhabitants of the Confederation. Hubbard estimated that the 76 planets averaged 178 billion people each. The people were killed and the Thetans (or spirits) gathered, frozen in a mixture of glycol and alcohol, and brought to Earth where they were placed near volcanoes that were exploded with hydrogen bombs. The thetans were gathered on 'electronic ribbons,' packaged together as clusters and given 36 days of hypnotic implanting, to render them servile and incapable of decision. These hypnotic implants supposedly contained the symbols of Christianity and all the social, religious and technological phenomena which have since ensued. According to Hubbard, Christianity is simply an implant and Christ an 'invention.'[9]

The subdued spirits are called body Thetans. A cluster is

a collection of body Thetans containing a leader and an 'alternate' leader. The cluster conceives itself to be an individual. According to Hubbard's secret teaching, everyone on Earth is in fact a collection of such clusters (everyone doing OT3 will find 'hundreds' of body Thetans – many believed that they found millions).

On OT3, the individual finds body Thetans by locating any sensation of pressure or mass in his or her body. This is addressed 'telepathically' as a cluster, and is supposedly brought to relive the cluster-making incident of 75 million years ago. After this, the individual body Thetans should be available to relive either the same incident or the incident of entry into this universe. This is called Incident One, and supposedly occurred four quadrillion years ago. This incident is described in the materials with the words 'Loud snap – waves of light – chariot comes out, turns left and right – cherub comes out – blows horn, comes close – shattering series of snaps – cherub fades back (retreats) – blackness dumped on Thetan.' In spite of Hubbard's insistence on clear definition of all terms, most scientologists are unaware of the proper biblical meaning for cherubim.

A Scientologist may spend days or years dealing with body Thetans. Scientology materials of different dates assert that at the end of OT 3 the individual will be 'stably exterior' (from his body), free from 'overwhelm' (nothing will ever again emotionally overwhelm him), and have total recall of his entire round of incarnations from four quadrillion years ago to the present. Secret materials seen only by those selling the course give the 'end phenomenon' or result as more simply a 'big win' urging that the person be put onto the next course – where they pay by the hour – quickly.

Of course, OT3 is in substantial disagreement with

conventional geology. Geologists hold that almost all of the volcanoes listed by Hubbard and both of his landing stages – Hawaii and Los Palmas – came into being far more recently than 75 million years ago. On a simple point of logic, it seems strange that none of these volcanoes were damaged by the explosion of the hydrogen bombs. Hubbard was taking barbiturates and drinking heavily when he wrote this material, according to letters he wrote at the time that are kept from Scientologists by the management of the cult.

Through OT3, Hubbard exploited the traditional belief in demon possession, and induced multiple personality disorder in his followers. It is not surprising that a number of Scientologists have either committed suicide or ended up in psychiatric hospitals. Scientologists pay tens, even hundreds, of thousands of dollars to achieve the supernatural powers promised them by the cult. Several thousand former Scientologists who have taken these courses can attest that the techniques are completely ineffective, leading only to progressive dissociation from reality. The first of his aides to visit Hubbard in Los Palmas was horrified that he was subsisting on a diet drawn from a shelf of drug bottles.

Hubbard suffered another in a long series of illnesses while 'researching' OT3. He was a heavy smoker, consuming as many as a hundred cigarettes a day, so was susceptible to respiratory infections. Questions were being asked in the British parliament by the time OT3 was completed, and Hubbard was to be declared an illegal alien and forbidden entry. He decided to become stateless while the heat was on, and, with his newly formed Sea Project, he took to the waves.

At its inception, the Sea Project numbered only nineteen loyal Scientologists, but with the publicity given by the world's press, membership rose rapidly. The Sea Project became the Sea Organisation, and by the end of the 1960s, Hubbard was travelling the Mediterranean with a retinue of hundreds of sailor-suited followers aboard several creaking old vessels. The largest of these had previously been a cattle ferry.

In 1968 in Corfu, a Sunday Times journalist watched as members of the cult were hurled headlong into the waters from the deck of Hubbard's ship Apollo. This betokened a new, tough era in Scientology. The slightest infringement of counselling procedure would lead to over boarding or to confinement in the pitch-black, rat-infested, fetid chain-lockers. Exulting in his power, Hubbard even published his photographs of over boarding.

By 1974, Hubbard's ragged fleet had been denied re-entry to most of the Mediterranean ports. In Madeira, locals had even pelted Hubbard's flagship with rocks. Hubbard decided to head home, and crossed the Atlantic to establish his new headquarters in Clearwater, Florida.

Hubbard ordered his legal department to make it safe for him to appear in public without being given a handful of subpoenas from the many people now suing his cult. He retreated to the California desert to fulfil a lifetime's ambition. Hubbard made movies about himself and Scientology. In the baking heat, a frantic crew danced attendance on the belligerent, overweight creator of Scientology. They produced a series of poorly acted, garish shorts.

Ron and Mary Sue Hubbard had four children. Ron Hubbard had announced that their oldest son, Quentin, would succeed him as leader of Scientology, even before the lad entered his teens. Quentin had achieved the highest level in Scientology. He was one of only 24 Class XII auditors and a graduate of all of the Operating Thetan levels. But to his father's disdain, Quentin was gay. And homosexuality is decried and forbidden in Scientology. At the end of October 1976, Quentin was found, comatose, in a parked car in Las Vegas. The engine was still running. He died two weeks later, without regaining consciousness. Quentin was 22 years old. There can be no greater indictment of Hubbard's purported bridge to complete mental and spiritual health.

Scientologists have been involved in various criminal activities. Eleven, including Hubbard's wife Mary Sue, were imprisoned in the US for infiltrating government agencies and stealing files, including Interpol files on terrorism. During the course of these activities Scientologists bugged and burgled government offices. Scientology is well known for its tireless campaigns against its critics. For instance, Hubbard ordered that a cartoonist be ruined for mentioning Scientology in a single cartoon. According to the private investigator who ran the campaign for Scientology, £100,000 was spent on following Sunday Times journalist Russell Miller. Author Paulette Cooper was framed for a bomb threat by Scientology.

Hubbard's lawyers worked away to make his return to public life possible. Just as the coast seemed clear, a huge scandal broke. In 1977, in the largest raid in its history, the FBI pounced on Scientology facilities in Los Angeles and Washington, DC. Hubbard's response to government concern about his organisation in 1966 had been the formation of the Guardian's Office under the control of his wife, Mary Sue. The Guardian's Office had taken over public relations, legal and intelligence functions for the Church of Scientology. The intelligence agency, known as the Information Bureau, housed two departments, B-1 and B-2. The second was concerned with the collection of publicly available material about critics, called 'overt data collection.' The trouble came through the activities of B-1, which was involved in 'covert data collection.' For covert read illegal.

Following Hubbard's specific orders – many of which were exhibited in the ensuing legal case – the Guardian's Office collected information about its opponents, and ran vicious harassment campaigns to silence criticism. The downfall of the Guardian's Office came with its infiltration of America's tax authority, the Internal Revenue Service. Scientology agents forged IRS credentials, and over a protracted period stole hundreds of thousands of documents from a variety of US government agencies. These files ranged from John Wayne's tax records to Interpol files on terrorism. Hubbard's wife and ten other members of the Guardian's Office were given prison sentences for crimes including breaking and entering, burglary, theft, kidnapping and false imprisonment. The war against critics of Scientology was revealed in the international media. Following Hubbard's orders, Scientology had run smear campaigns against many individuals and infiltrated numerous organisations ranging from the Better Business Bureau to the US Coast Guard. A Scientologist police lieutenant was disciplined for using FBI computers to prevent the capture of the felons. Prosecutions in Canada followed. Here the cult had infiltrated the police force and the Ontario state legislature to steal some forty filing cabinets worth of documents. This led to the first conviction of a religious organisation in Canadian history.

There was no denying the extent of these intelligence operations. Hubbard went into hiding and ordered the dismantling of the Guardian's Office by his Messengers. With the formation of the Sea Organisation, Hubbard had promoted himself to the rank of Commodore. The children aboard his ship had become the Commodore's Messenger Organisation. These loyal teenagers and twenty-something's were now given the task of purging the old guard.

Hubbard ended his days in Creston, California. He was two months short of his seventy-fifth birthday, and by the account of those who saw him a very sick man given to blistering rages. Hubbard's health had been poor for many years, in spite of his claims to have found a psychotherapeutic cure for most of the very ailments he suffered from. Since the early 1970s, he had been attended by a nurse. He was unable to quit smoking and also took a roster of prescription drugs, including a decoagulating medicine to prevent the recurrence of a pulmonary embolism which had already threatened his life a decade before his death. His teeth had long since rotted away. In the end, the raging and rambling old man succumbed to a stroke. News of his death, on January 24th, 1986, was overshadowed by the space shuttle disaster. Although Hubbard had also suffered a stroke a week before his death, Scientology officials claimed that he had been lucid when he amended his will insisting that there should be no autopsy. His body was quickly cremated, and the ashes scattered at sea.

Following his death, an album of pop music made under Hubbard's direction, and with the collaboration of Scientologist jazz superstar Chick Corea, was released. The leading British music journal Melody Maker, summed up the album saying 'You're supposed to eat vegetables, not listen to them.'

Hubbard left behind a fortune of over 600 million dollars. He had probably spent as much again, all of it collected from his followers. Travelling over Hubbard's Scientology Bridge costs hundreds of thousands of pounds. A single hour of counselling can cost a thousand dollars. Some Scientologists have lost their homes and businesses to pay for increasingly expensive courses. While being promised that through Scientology they will regain their ability to make their own decisions – their 'self-determinism' – the courses actually lead to unquestioning acceptance of Hubbard's belief system, and the erosion of independent thought.

During the 1980s, the Church of Scientology was at the centre of several remarkable court cases. The cult brought suit against defecting member Gerald Armstrong who had taken thousands of documents from the very archive of Hubbard's life that he had created at Hubbard's order.

After a spectacular four-week trial, Judge Breckenridge ruled against the cult saying that while assembling the documents relating to Hubbard's life 'Armstrong began to see that Hubbard and the Organization had continuously lied about Hubbard's past, his credentials, and his accomplishments.'

The Judge added that after the suit was filed against Armstrong he had been 'the subject of harassment, including being followed and surveilled by individuals who admitted employment by Plaintiff [Scientology]; being assaulted by one of these individuals; being struck bodily by a car driven by one of these individuals; having two attempts made by said individuals apparently to involve Defendant Armstrong in a freeway automobile accident; having said individuals come onto Defendant Armstrong's property, spy in his windows, create disturbances, and upset his neighbours. During trial when it appeared that Howard Schomer (a former Scientologist) might be called as a defence witness, the Church engaged in a somewhat sophisticated effort to suppress his testimony.'

More generally, Judge Breckenridge ruled 'In addition to violating and abusing its own member's civil rights, the organization over the years with its "Fair Game" doctrine has harassed and abused those persons not in the Church whom it perceives as enemies. The organization clearly is schizophrenic and paranoid, and this bizarre combination seems to be a reflection of its founder LRH [L. Ron Hubbard]. The evidence portrays a man who has been virtually a pathological liar when it comes to his history, background, and achievements. The writings and documents in evidence additionally reflect his egoism, greed, avarice, lust for power, and vindictiveness and aggressiveness against persons perceived by him to be disloyal or hostile. At the same time it appears that he is charismatic and highly capable of motivating, organizing, controlling, manipulating, and inspiring his adherents. He has been referred to during the trial as a "genius," a "revered person," a man who was "viewed by his followers in awe." Obviously, he is and has been a very complex person, and that complexity is further reflected in his alter ego, the Church of Scientology. Notwithstanding protestations to the contrary, this court is satisfied that LRH runs the Church in all ways through the Sea Organization, his role of Commodore, and the Commodore's Messengers. He has, of course, chosen to go into "seclusion," but he maintains contact and control through the top messengers. Seclusion has its light and dark side too. It adds to his mystique, and yet shields him from accountability and subpoena or service of summons.

He continued, 'LRH's wife, Mary Sue Hubbard is also a plaintiff herein. On the one hand she certainly appeared to be a pathetic individual. She was forced from her post as Controller, convicted and imprisoned as a felon, and deserted by her husband. On the other hand her credibility leaves much to be desired. She struck the familiar pose of not seeing, hearing, or knowing any evil. Yet she was the head of the Guardian Office for years and among other things, authored the infamous order "GO [Guardian's Order] 121669" which directed culling of supposedly confidential P.C. [Preclear] files/folders for the purposes of internal security. In her testimony she expressed the feelings that defendant by delivering the documents, writings, letters to his attorneys, subjected her to mental rape ... The court is satisfied that he [Armstrong] did not unreasonably intrude upon Mrs. Hubbard's privacy under the circumstances ... It is, of course, rather ironic that the person who authorized G.O. order 121669 should complain about an invasion of privacy. The practice of culling supposedly confidential "P.C. folders or files" to obtain information for purposes of intimidation and/or harassment is repugnant and outrageous. The Guardian's Office, which plaintiff headed, was no respecter of anyone's civil rights, particularly that of privacy.'

It has often been charged that Scientology splits up families. This stems from the practise of 'disconnection,' whereby Scientologists are forbidden to speak to anyone critical of Scientology.

On the heels of this judgment came another in a child custody case. In England, family cases are heard privately, but Justice Latey was so outraged by the evidence he heard that he chose to make his ruling public. Although he could only rule with regard to the residence of the children – who were returned to their non-Scientologist mother – the judge gave his opinion of the cult in no uncertain terms:

'Scientology is both immoral and socially obnoxious ... In my judgment it is corrupt, sinister and dangerous. It is corrupt because it is based on lies and deceit and has as its real objective money and power for Mr. Hubbard, his wife and those close to him at the top. It is sinister because it indulges in infamous practices both to its adherents who do not toe the line unquestioningly and to those who criticise or oppose it. It is dangerous because it is out to capture people, especially children and impressionable young people, and indoctrinate and brainwash them so that they become the unquestioning captives and tools of the cult, withdrawn from ordinary thought, living and relationships with others.'

These cases highlighted the dreadful conditions imposed upon Scientology staff members, who often work for as much as 90 hours a week for less than five pounds. Scientology is governed by the Sea Organisation, members of which wear pseudo-naval uniform, including campaign ribbons. Often, they are allowed to see their children only once every two weeks. These children are brought up in the Cadet Organisation, where they are taught absolute obedience to Scientology and a fear of the outside or 'wog' world, as Hubbard termed it.

When their production statistics sag, Sea Organisation members are put on a diet of rice and beans, sometimes for months on end. Miscreants are moved to pigs berthing. If this punishment fails, the offender is put into the Rehabilitation Project Force or RPF. Membership of the RPF usually lasts for several months, but can last for as much as two years. RPFers eat table scraps, sleep even shorter hours than the rest of the staff, may not speak unless spoken to, work long hours at menial tasks such as toilet cleaning, must obey all orders without question or hesitation, and spend five hours a day confessing the evil purposes of their supposed previous incarnations. The RPF is a testimony to the mind control techniques of Scientology. It is a sophisticated version of Mao's infamous Chinese thought reform programmes.

Through the 1980s, rulings followed in other civil cases.

Tens of millions of dollars were awarded to former members. Most organisations would have crumbled under such pressure, but under the direction of its youthful new leader, David Miscavige, the cult fought every ruling. The legal tactic was simple – deluge the opposition with hundreds of motions and counter-motions: create a paper mountain of interminable legal pleadings. Given resources of hundreds of millions of dollars it proved possible to outlast most opponents. Judgment amounts were reduced by the simple expedient of transferring assets from any corporation that had been sued. In this way, the former mother church, the Church of Scientology of California, which had once boasted assets of hundreds of millions of dollars, pleaded poverty when ordered to recompense former member Lawrence Wollersheim to the tune of two and a half million dollars. Many weary litigants settled out of court, signing contracts which prohibited them from making any further public comment. In the largest of these settlements, Boston lawyer Michael Flynn was given $5 million to silence his clients.

Author Jon Atack was beaten into bankruptcy through a series of court cases, unable to fund his defence and tangled by legal stratagems. No evidence was ever heard in these cases, which ran for a period of eight years, only an elaborate web of pre-trial motions. Ultimately, Atack made undertakings not to repeat a passage relating to Narconon in his booklet The Total Freedom Trap, and not to copy or quote from specific Scientology documents. In a libel case, where his defence was dismissed on a technicality without any evidence being heard, Atack was ordered not to repeat a paragraph relating to the headmistress of a school run on Scientology principles in his book A Piece of Blue Sky. Inevitably, this led to claims that the book itself had been banned.

Atack was not alone in receiving attention through the courts and from private detectives hired by the cult. According to the private detective who ran the campaign for the cult, £100,000 was spent on following Sunday Times journalist Russell Miller around the globe. Author Paulette Cooper had even been framed for a bomb threat by Scientology.

The cult sidesteps criticism, attacking the critic rather than responding to the allegation. Sometimes, when a critic has the resources to fight back, this mud throwing leads the cult into trouble. In Canada, barrister Casey Hill took exception to the vigorous campaign mounted against him by the cult. After years in the courts, Hill eventually won a judgment against the cult in 1995. The judges were outraged by the cult's attempts to silence Hill and summed up a lengthy ruling with the words, 'Every aspect of this case demonstrates the very real and persistent malice of Scientology.'

With the birth of the Internet, the campaign had to be waged against numerous new critics. Raids followed in Finland, Holland and the USA, with the cult demanding protection of its commercial copyrights through the courts. The Dutch European courts have proved more resilient than the American ones in protecting their citizens' rights to free speech. The budget for private detectives must have been enormous. In Germany there was government action to restrict the growth of Scientology. A French court case revealed activities very similar to those of the Guardian's Office two decades earlier. Members of the cult were briefly imprisoned. In Greece a raid of Scientology offices revealed the possession of documents belonging to the Greek Intelligence services. Nonetheless, Scientology managed to achieve tax-exempt status in the US in 1993. No explanation has been offered by the officials who awarded exemption, save that they were ordered to do so.

It is 17 years since Judge Latey exposed Scientology as a dangerous cult, but it continues to masquerade as a religion in Britain. This despite the refusal of religious status by the Charity Commissioners.

In 1992, the European Council adopted a resolution saying that 'information ... on the nature and activities of sects and new religious movements, should ... be widely circulated to the general public,' and that 'Independent bodies should be set up to collect and circulate information.' Scientology was mentioned in the body of the discussion. Nothing has been done to implement this resolution in Britain.

NOTES

1. Hubbard, *The Research and Discovery Series*, vol.1, first editon 1980, Scientology Publications Org, p.124.
2. L.Ron Hubbard, *Conditions of Space Time Energy*, 1952, PDC lecture 18.
3. Sigmund Freud, Clarke Lectures 1-3, in *Two Short Accounts of Psychoanalysis*, Penguin Books, London, 1962.
4. See Atack, Jon 'Never believe a hypnotist – an investigation of L. Ron Hubbard's statements about hypnosis and its relationship to his Dianetics,' 1995, for an exhaustive account of Hubbard's admissions about his use of hypnosis.
5. *Dianetics: The Modern Science of Mental Health*, p.363 original edition, p.389 in later editions; see also *Research and Discovery* volume 1, first edition, pp.124, 305, 313; *Research and Discovery* volume 4, p.37.
6. See Atack, Jon *Possible Origins for Dianetics and Scien-*

tology, 1995 and Atack, Jon Hubbard and the Occult, 1995.

7. *Modern Management Technology Defined*, under the entry for Church of American Science.

8. 'Expanded Gita' in Hubbard, *The Creation of Human Ability*, 1954.

9. Hubbard, *Resistive Cases – Former Therapy*, Class VIII course, HCOB 23 September 1968.

For further information, or to contact
Richard and Bonnie, go to:

www.escapeint.org